SANTA MARIA PUBLIC LIBRARY 06/08

the
DIAPER-
FREE
BABY

$\frac{10}{11/1}$

$\frac{ILL\ 10}{11\ 1}$

the DIAPER-FREE BABY

The Natural Toilet Training Alternative

Christine Gross-Loh

REGAN

An Imprint of HarperCollins*Publishers*

All photography by Dan Loh, except for page 201, by Denis Gopan.

HarperCollins books may be purchased for educational, business, or sales promotional use. For information please write: Special Markets Department, HarperCollins Publishers, 10 East 53rd Street, New York, NY 10022.

For editorial inquiries, please contact Regan, 10100 Santa Monica Blvd., 10th floor, Los Angeles, CA 90067.

DiaperFreeBaby is a trademark of DiaperFreeBaby, Inc.

FIRST EDITION

Designed by Kris Tobiassen

Library of Congress Cataloging-in-Publication Data

Gross-Loh, Christine.
  The diaper-free baby: the natural toilet training alternative/
  Christine Gross-Loh.—1st ed.
      p.   cm.
  ISBN-13: 978-0-06-122970-1
  ISBN-10: 0-06-122970-9
    1. Toilet training. 2. Parent and infant. 3. Interpersonal communication in infants. I. Title.

HQ770.5.G76 2007
649'.62—dc22   2006050370

07 08 09 10 11 DIX/RRD 10 9 8 7 6 5 4 3 2 1

This book is dedicated to my two little
diaper-free babies, Benjamin and Daniel,
who, from the moment of birth,
opened my heart to all that babies
and children have to say to us.

CONTENTS

FOREWORD

By Melinda Rothstein and Rachel Milgroom, cofounders of DiaperFreeBaby™

We both entered motherhood expecting to change years of diapers, just like every parent we had ever known. Melinda thought of taking her one-week-old son to the bathroom when she knew he was about to go, but dismissed it immediately as ridiculous because she'd never known anyone who did it. Rachel was dedicated to the idea that a child should be helped to learn to use the toilet at a young age, but thought that meant starting at around a year old and that anything younger would be impossible and incredibly messy. Only after being encouraged by other parents did we start to consider an alternative to full-time diapering.

What these other parents told us is this: Our babies are born ready to communicate that they need to use the potty, and the time spent taking a baby to the potty can be fun. Half of the world's children are out of diapers by the end of their first year, yet many of the children in American society remain in diapers well into their third and fourth years. We learned that it is possible to practice elimination communication (EC) regardless of differences in work schedule or parenting style—from a few times per week to many times per day, one caregiver to many, starting at birth or starting later in the first year. We came to understand that parents in an exclusively diapering culture need assistance as they shift their mindsets about elimination and diapering.

Once we understood that babies are aware of their elimination needs and have ways of communicating those needs, it made perfect sense to us to help them use the potty. Both of us started our elimination communication journey with our children at approximately the same time as Christine did with her second son, Daniel. We influenced each other's choices and provided support to each other as we learned. Through frequent contact via e-mail with other families we learned practical day-to-day tips and started a local playgroup for families practicing EC. From these relationships we learned about our infants' innate intelligence and increased our ability to understand when they were communicating their needs.

At the time, none of us had any idea how much EC was going to add to our lives. We definitely had no inkling that we'd be so enriched by it that we'd become involved in the effort to publicize the practice to parents everywhere. The international EC support organization, DiaperFreeBaby™, was born out of our desire to help other families meet for support and sharing. We knew that families would be happy to have a way to connect with each other, but we were completely surprised by the level of international media interest.

This growing interest makes it clear that it is time for Christine's book, and we're thrilled that so many parents will now have the opportunity to explore EC for their families. Christine is the perfect person to write this book, as she has both the loving perspective of an EC parent and the professional skill to present the information. From our first playgroup with Christine, her perspectives on elimination communication and parenting, as well as her own gentle nature, have been indispensable to us personally and to the parenting community as a whole. She has been totally committed to the social movement that has occurred since we started DiaperFreeBaby support groups, including the exponential growth of the New York City DiaperFreeBaby group that she started. Now she has written a book that is sure to inspire you to start practicing EC if you have not already begun.

Christine expertly shares real stories as well as practical tips and guidance for integrating EC into your family life. We hope that you will view this book as a DiaperFreeBaby meeting in your pocket and hope it will enrich your life as well.

the DIAPER-FREE BABY

1.

What Is EC, and Why Should I Do It with My Baby?

Diapers. We're so used to thinking of them as the ultimate symbol of babyhood that the thought of a baby without diapers seems awfully strange. It's practically a rite of passage for parents to get their toddlers and preschoolers out of diapers. Advice abounds on getting your two- or three-year-old to ditch those diapers and begin to learn to go in a potty or toilet. The current trend is to let your child wait until he is "ready," and as a result, many parents find themselves involved in power struggles with their toddlers and preschoolers day after day because they missed crucial earlier windows of opportunity. The average toilet training age in the United States is now at an all-time high at around three years old. It makes sense, actually, that after a couple of years eliminating exclusively in diapers, a child will be inclined to hang on to them as long as he can. How odd it is, in fact, that our society expects a child to change gears midstream and suddenly stop using the diaper as a toilet when he has been doing so all his life!

Believe it or not, your child was not born wanting to go to the bathroom in a diaper. Like other mammals, human babies are born with the instinct not to soil themselves. It is not a natural or pleasant feeling for them to sit in their own waste; they are born aware of the sensation of going to the bathroom. Even the tiniest newborn will give off signs before and while she goes to the bathroom. This book is going to teach you how to read those signs, how to respond to them, and how to engage in a process of joyful communication with your baby at a pace that feels right for your family, whether this means once a day or more often. Through "elimination communication," or EC, your baby will benefit as you help her retain her bodily awareness and assist her with a basic biological need. The benefit for you? In addition to parenting a happier baby, you're likely to need fewer diapers overall—great for your wallet and for the environment!

For those who have spent time with older babies or toddlers who seem oblivious to a dirty diaper, the idea that they are born with the instinct not to soil themselves may seem preposterous. Being sprayed by newborn pee and poop as soon as a diaper comes off *during* diaper changes are a common occurrence throughout a baby's first weeks (another common rite of passage for most parents), but this happens less and less often as the baby grows older. Why? By putting our children in diapers and changing them only *after* they have gone, we condition our babies to use the diaper itself as a toilet!

Some people might think, so what? Isn't diapering a part of babyhood? Aren't diapers a sign of progress, modernity, and affluence? Perhaps that would be so if we did not expect our little ones to stop using diapers at some point in the first few years of their lives. Since this is the case, many parents are faced with double work: training a child to go to the bathroom in a diaper, and then training her to stop doing that and use a toilet instead! This means twice as much work for parents and twice as much adjustment for the child. The later this gets—especially if you're waiting for all the signs of "readiness" described by conventional toilet training experts—the more of an adjustment it can be for your child, and the more diaper changes, diapers, and diapering accessories you've gone through in the meantime. (If your child is training around age three, this means up to nine thousand diaper changes and diapers, over three thousand dollars in diapers alone [not to mention wipes and other accessories], and according to a *New York Times* article on elimination communication, a contribution to the twenty-two billion single-use, disposable diapers in U.S. landfills per year, to be exact!)

Of course, many children sail through conventional potty training just fine. But there are countless others who have trouble recognizing which muscles to use to hold or release pee or who just find it physically and emotionally difficult to let go of the diaper they have been used to all their lives. Even after some children become aware of the elimination sensation, they are still so accustomed to diapers that they actually request a diaper to put on before they go to the bathroom! Others simply take a long time to train, and their parents resort to pleading, bribes, stickers, M&Ms, videos, musical potties, and other such gimmicks. Still other children suffer from excruciating diaper rash, fiercely resist diaper changes, or otherwise find diapering to be an unpleasant experience the whole way through. They develop negative associations with anything having to do with diapering and elimination itself.

You're probably reading this book because you hope to avoid these scenarios, and EC fits in with your parenting philosophy and resonates with you for financial, environmental, or personal reasons. Read on to learn more about EC and why I recommend you consider practicing it with your baby.

ELIMINATION COMMUNICATION: A GENTLE ALTERNATIVE

Imagine what it would be like if your baby was so accustomed to the concept of using a toilet as, well, a toilet, that when it did come time to become completely toilet-independent, she took the process completely for granted, so that the transition was utterly smooth. Imagine if this toilet independence came about without bribes, struggles, resistance, or tantrums and was instead a natural, completely gentle, noncoercive process that your baby was fully participating in, so that as an infant, she would be able to let you know when she had to go to the bathroom, and by the time she was walking, she could toddle over to the toilet by herself just like she might toddle over to the kitchen if she were hungry. That's what happens in many families who practice EC with their babies.

EC is a lost art in our society. It is still practiced throughout the world, mostly in countries where disposable diapers are considered a luxury if they are available at all. In fact, there are many people out there who think that we are odd for relying on diapers so much. It's really diapers that are the new phenomenon—not EC. In the United States, some version of early potty training was practiced up until disposable diaper use became more widespread in the 1960s and '70s. Before this time, most children were out of diapers by age two, if not earlier. EC is still practiced in at least seventy-five countries,

 including China, India, Greenland, and Russia, and in many other parts of Africa, South America, and Asia. Because the children from many of these cultures have never had to lose the bodily awareness they were born with—mothers or caregivers simply hold babies away from them when they sense they need to go—most of them are toilet-independent incredibly early from our society's point of view. One study states that 50 percent of the world's children are toilet

trained by the age of one. Many internationally adopting parents are "startled" to find that their babies arrive already able to use the toilet, according to the *New York Times*. With statistics like these, the idea that toilet training shouldn't *begin* until age two or three, when the child meets the conditions of an arbitrary checklist for "readiness," seems more and more absurd.

But it's common for parents to be skeptical even in the face of all this evidence. Even if EC works and children are physically and emotionally capable of doing this, it still sounds utterly overwhelming for new parents in our society. We live in homes with carpets, we're constantly on the go, parents go back to work when babies are merely weeks old, and children are often in the care of nannies or day-care providers or relatives. How can EC really work in a modern Western society such as ours?

I'm here to say that EC can be accomplished. If EC is something you'd like to try, you are about to hear from many parents just like you who have done it with great success. This book is filled with their reassuring voices and the rich variety of their personal experiences. You'll learn how to practice EC in the way that is best for your family situation and preferences, with plenty of options to make it work for anyone in any situation. Whether you are a stay-at-home mom or dad or you are separated from your baby for long hours because of work, whether you use cloth diapers or disposable ones, whether you're starting with a tiny newborn or are coming to this with a baby who is six months, ten months, or well over a year old, there are guidelines in this book that will work for you.

EC HISTORY AND SUPPORT GROUPS

Although parents in our society have easy access to diapers and use them liberally with their babies and toddlers, this isn't the case for everyone. In much of the world, elimination communication is still the norm, as it always has been. Some of the most ardent advocates of EC have been influenced and inspired by time spent in a country where EC is the cultural norm.

Laurie Boucke, Linda Penn (Natec), and Ingrid Bauer all came to EC through their contacts with other cultures and went on to write on the subject for Western audiences. Bauer refers to infant pottying as "Natural Infant Hygiene" (NIH) and also coined the term *elimination communication.* Boucke, who has written several books, including *Infant Potty Training,* and is coauthoring several forthcoming medical studies on EC, says, "For years, I've emphasized that it's really important for parents to be presented with more than one option so they can make an informed decision" about whether to use diapers exclusively or to learn to recognize baby's elimination signals and assist her in using a potty or toilet.

EC became more well known through such advocacy, but only a relatively small group of Western parents were familiar with the concept. Most parents who embraced EC were drawn to it because of its close connection with attachment parenting principles.

Recently, however, the word has been spreading rapidly. Growing numbers of parents have been gathering in support groups to assist each other in the practice of EC. These support groups are so inspiring! In addition to groups people have started on their own, many groups have been formed under the umbrella of a wonderful nonprofit organization called DiaperFreeBaby. Founded in 2004 by two of my close friends, Melinda Rothstein and Rachel Milgroom, DiaperFreeBaby's membership has just ballooned. At the end of its second year there were support groups or practicing families in nearly every state as well as in fourteen countries, and growth has continued to be exponential thanks to sustained public and media interest in EC.

I myself participated in one of the first EC support groups with Melinda, Rachel, and a few other friends. During our monthly meetings, we all came together with our babies and shared tips, which was a really great experience for us. It became obvious that parents all over the country who sought EC guidance would love to share their experiences with each other, and thanks to Melinda and Rachel's dream of bringing this camaraderie to parents everywhere, DiaperFreeBaby was born.

I am now a Mentor for my local support group. Mentors bring parents together in a forum where they can talk to each other about the daily practice of EC. This sort of forum is so important when you are practicing something that isn't all that commonly done. I urge you to go to a local meeting if you can. You will see adorable babies gently being assisted to use the potty; and you will also be introduced to real EC'ing gear, such as portable potties, split crotch pants, tiny training pants, and so forth—all designed to make EC'ing easier for parents in our society. Best of all, however, you will meet other parents like yourself.

But if you are not near an active support group or just want more guidance at home, this book was written just for you. I encourage you to think of it as your own portable support group, filled with the voices of many parents at all stages of the EC journey! And, of course, I hope that my own story will serve as inspiration to you as well.

MY JOURNEY TO EC

Chances are you're reading this book because you've heard the media buzz about all these parents taking their babies to the potty. Maybe you think it's far-fetched but are intrigued and wondering if this is something you can really do.

I know how it feels. I was also one of those intrigued but doubtful parents when I first learned about EC while expecting my first son, Benjamin. Like most people who use diapers, my primary concern was to get the most absorbent diapers I could find—diapers that could withstand several hours without leaking. I'd heard about diaper changes, and I dreaded them. When I heard that there were parents out there who practiced something called "elimination communication," I was, frankly, shocked. The very notion that a tiny baby could use the potty seemed ludicrous and completely odd to me, even though I myself had actually watched three-month-old infants being pottied when I was studying abroad! That is how ingrained the idea that toilet learning is reserved for two- to three-year-olds is in our society. I ignored the newborn spray, tried to get through those diaper changes, and stocked my bulging diaper bag with tons of diapers and wipes whenever I was on the go.

Yet over time I found that I was aware of my baby's elimination patterns. I realized that as he grew older, he often went hours in the afternoon with a dry diaper. I observed that he would wet more frequently in the mornings, and that he was very obvious about when he was having a bowel movement. Even so, it really didn't occur to me to put him on the potty at those times even though I knew about EC. I'm not sure why not, except that maybe in my mind, I saw it as something that would be totally time-consuming and impractical, and I knew absolutely no one who was doing it. In the end, it was my child himself who led me to EC.

When Benjamin was just over a year old, my mother (who grew up in Korea) bought him a potty. My first reaction was complete indignation! I thought I, a hip, modern parent, knew better than she, and that "better" now meant waiting until he was two or three, not starting with a preverbal thirteen-month-old! I even thought that early pottying could be harmful somehow. But before returning the potty to my mom, I decided to sit little Benjamin on it just for fun, because it seemed so cute, and he was certainly fascinated. Well, he peed in the potty right away!

I was astounded! And even more astounded when he repeated this every time I sat him on it throughout that day and the next. I began to realize that he had been waiting for me to understand that he wanted to go to the bathroom outside of a diaper. He had been watching all of us using toilets and was eager to join in. I finally tapped into all the EC resources I'd taken note of, adapted those methods for my "late-start" EC'ing baby, found some support online, and within a week or two, he was completely out of diapers.

Now, Benjamin's story is a bit unusual. It's rare for a child to retain that bodily awareness for so long, and I often hesitate to share this story because of how young Benjamin was when he "graduated" (became completely toilet-independent with no "misses"—EC-speak for accidents). While getting out of diapers earlier than the U.S. average is something that happens with a lot of EC'ed children, it's not the main point of EC at all, and I wouldn't want parents to embark on this journey with that primary goal. You see, this method is not about getting your baby potty trained sooner than anyone else's child. It's about the process of communication, not the result. There's no time frame, no deadline as to when your child should be fully out of diapers.

But I do share this story with people because it highlights a couple of things: children can be ready much earlier than we think; EC can totally enhance their self-esteem and sense of independence by allowing them to use a toilet when they are so young and imitative (rather than when they are going through the resistant and strong-willed twos); and because it really shows that, contrary to popular belief, early pottying doesn't mean that it will be a messy, drawn-out,

My son Daniel, one year old, on the toilet

and stressful experience. The gentle principles of EC made for the most seamless, beautifully bonding toileting experience I could ever have hoped to have with my toddler!

With my second son, Daniel, we started practicing EC when he was around three weeks old. Now, the important thing I like to point out about my experience with him is that even if you begin with a tiny baby, this doesn't mean you're going to be a slave to his signals and whims to use the toilet all the time. EC turns this mentality on its head; recognizing your child's need to go to the bathroom is truly no different from recognizing his sleep or hunger cues, as you're going to learn from reading this book. It's no different from what any loving and attentive parent would do to try to figure out what his or her baby is communicating.

Because Daniel had health issues during part of his infancy, I made a conscious decision to put EC on the back burner with him and practice it only occasionally. Thus, we did it very part-time—as little as once a week for the first few months of his life. Later we ramped up to catching poops only, with just an occasional pee, and finally practiced it more full-time when he was a bit older. He graduated at around seventeen months. Even following EC part-time, I like to point out, results in a baby who is not completely diaper trained and who recognizes that you are going to assist him with his desire not to sit in his own waste. You are still engaging in the important process of EC—communication—with your baby. He has the opportunity to retain his awareness of the muscles that control his elimination and the ability to let you know when he has to go.

Even with just my own two sons, I've had a real variety of EC experiences: early-start, late-start, full-time, part-time. Between my story and those of the many inspiring parents featured in this book, I am certain that you will find something that works for your family.

INTRODUCING THE THREE TRACKS

Because I've found that so many parents practice EC to varying degrees, I've decided to introduce the concept of three tracks, which I'll be referring to throughout the book: full-time EC, part-time EC, and occasional EC. You will probably find that one of these approaches initially appeals to you more than others, but they are not hard and fast categories. Most EC'ers fluctuate between categories all the time without even consciously thinking about it. I've spelled the tracks out explicitly in hopes that these concepts will help you navigate this book more smoothly.

Full-time EC'ers, in general, start following EC soon after birth (although you can certainly start practicing EC full-time at any stage of your child's infancy or early toddlerhood). Usually there is at least one parent or primary caregiver present with the baby at all times, and the baby is often worn in a sling during the early months. Full-time EC'ers practice EC as much as they can throughout the day and night, aiming to provide their baby with the opportunity to go to the bathroom as many times as they think he needs. Full-time EC'ers, like all EC'ers, are usually most comfortable first practicing EC at home. Over time, they may choose to practice it out of the house as well, although there are plenty of families who make a point to practice EC only when they are near home. The babies of full-time EC'ers are often diaper-free early on (if they ever wear diapers at all). This doesn't mean that their parents catch every pee or never encounter a wet training pant. However, the intensive nature of full-time EC means that parents will usually get to a point pretty early on when they are so in tune with their babies that they catch most pees and all poops, with very few misses. It becomes as second nature to them as noticing when their baby is hungry or sleepy.

Part-time EC'ers catch whatever they are able to, but don't practice EC all the time. They might focus on EC during the mornings, for instance, when they are able to spend uninterrupted time with their baby, or for an hour or two in the evening. They might be catching all of their baby's bowel movements; in fact, quite a few EC'ers start with bowel movements because they are so predictable and it is so rewarding for parent and baby not to clean a poopy bottom and diaper. There are even EC'ers who focus only on bowel movements during most of infancy, choosing to approach pees later, when their child is older.

Occasional EC'ers practice EC only occasionally. This could mean catching as little as one pee a day, or even less often. It can even mean offering the baby a chance to use the potty at a time when the diaper is going to be off anyway—during a diaper change, for instance, or right before bath time. Occasional EC'ers may also use diapers nearly all the time without even using a potty, but make an effort to cue their baby, to recognize his signals, and to keep communicating with him about elimination even if it is happening in a diaper. If they change his diaper pretty quickly afterward so that he doesn't have to sit in a dirty diaper, and if they talk to him about the process as much as possible, there is a really good chance that the baby will be able to retain his bodily awareness of elimination, which will result in a smoother transition to being diaper-free later in infancy or toddlerhood, when there are renewed opportunities to practice EC in other ways.

As this book will show you, EC can be as simple as offering your baby a chance to use the toilet once a day, when her diaper happens to be off, or as intensive as aiming to catch a majority of your baby's output. There is a huge range of experiences out there that qualify as elimination communication. What they all have in common is the parents' desire to connect with their baby, to understand what their baby is communicating, and to show their baby that they are there to lovingly and gently help him meet his needs. Remember that the wonderful thing about EC is that it offers you flexibility depending on what suits your and your baby's needs best. You don't have to commit to one track rather than the other—just go with the flow. As you'll see, there are a variety of EC'ing parents out there whose experiences are sure to resonate with you.

MYTHS AND MISCONCEPTIONS

I encounter a range of reactions when people find out that my little ones were in underwear when they were so young. Although most people are intrigued and amazed, they are also often skeptical that EC could ever work for their own families. Below, I've listed and addressed the most commonly cited reasons why parents believe the EC lifestyle won't work for them.

1. "I think it's training the parent, not the child."

EC'ers hear this a lot. If you think that learning to tell when your baby is hungry or sleepy is "training" you, then yes, learning to read your baby's cues that she needs to go to the bathroom could also be considered parent training. However, I prefer to emphasize that it's not about training at all. EC is not toilet training the way you train an older child to use the toilet. It's engaging in communication and becoming in tune with your wonderful baby by responding to a basic need. There's nothing negative about being "trained" in this way. Above all else, realize that focusing on "training" leads us away from what EC is really about. EC is not so much about the *result* (a toilet-independent child) as it is about the *process* of communication.

2. "Wouldn't it just be easier for my child to train on his own when he is older?"

Of course, all children eventually become toilet-independent as older toddlers or preschoolers, and their joy and pride in this is a wonderful thing to see. But EC'ed babies have the opportunity to experience the independence of fully understanding their bodies well before that, and the transition to the toilet is often smoother for children who have never been exclusively diaper-reliant. If you have ever seen an eight-month-old signal that she has to use the toilet, or a one-year-old run over to a potty and use it on his own while delighting in the whole process, you will have no doubt that EC'ed children experience a unique feeling of self-sufficiency and self-awareness.

3. "I don't want a mess all over my house—isn't EC difficult to do in Western society?"

Some parents will make changes to their house—taking up the rugs temporarily, perhaps focusing on EC only when they happen to be in one room, and so on. The initial learning period does not last very long. As you and your baby learn to connect, you will have fewer misses with which to deal. Besides, you'd likely have misses if you were conventionally toilet training a child anyway. Remember, you can always use diapers as backup or even full-time if it helps you feel more relaxed. Plenty of parents follow EC without going completely diaper-free.

4. "Isn't EC kind of weird—like you're hovering over your child, waiting for her to pee or poop?"

About the hovering, many parents are in close proximity to their newborn babies. It's a misconception that EC parents spend all their time hovering and waiting for the next pee or poop. Parents quickly pick up on their baby's elimination patterns just as they pick up on their baby's need to eat or sleep. They don't have to think about it all the time. In addition, parents often find that their EC'ed babies often begin consolidating their pees and poops and eliminate less frequently than an exclusively diapered baby.

There are certainly new challenges to EC'ing a mobile baby. If you have a crawling, exploring, older baby, it can be difficult to keep her close by no matter how hard you try. But I—like many EC'ing parents—found that being so in tune with my baby meant that sometimes I just "knew" he had to go to the bathroom even if I was in another room. That is the nature of the awareness you cultivate during this journey.

5. "Why should my baby have to communicate her elimination? She's just a baby. Why can't I just let her relax and use a diaper?"

Once you recognize that your baby was born with the innate awareness not to soil her own diaper, you'll realize that she is not being forced to communicate or do anything beyond her natural abilities. In fact, by ignoring a baby's elimination signals, we're asking her to tune out a natural instinct and instead endure something she likely finds unpleasant. EC'ed babies are so comfortable going to the bathroom—they often seem to take it very much for granted—that it's quite obvious we're not asking anything of a baby by engaging in EC. Besides, what could be more comfortable and easy for a baby than going diaper-free?

6. "I have older children to take care of too."

Older children get used to interruptions, and they quickly learn that you are as present for them as you can be even while feeding or changing a baby. Older brothers and sisters can also be intuitive and communicative with their younger siblings, even more so than their parents! I recall the many times, when I wasn't being perceptive, that Benjamin would let me

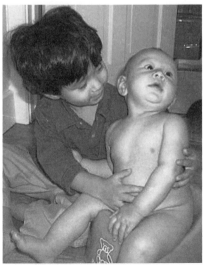

Siblings love to help out. Here, my son Benjamin helps hold Daniel up on the potty.

know that baby Daniel had to go to the bathroom. Brothers and sisters are also great models; babies learn so much from watching their siblings use the toilet. Finally, the enhanced communication your EC'ed baby experiences with you is something your children will experience between one another as well.

7. "I work outside the home."

EC is about communication, and anyone can learn to communicate with a child. If your partner, relatives, or caregiver are reluctant to try EC because they don't understand it, give them some time. Your baby may also figure out how to communicate to her caregiver as she gets older. If you find that your baby is only going to be EC'ed when you are around, that's fine too; she can switch between diapers and the potty very easily, just as babies can learn to use both the breast and the bottle.

8. "I am too overwhelmed."

EC can be practiced part-time, just as I did with Daniel during his infancy. At those times, my goal was simply to be vigilant and to help Daniel retain his bodily awareness by changing him as soon as he went, verbally acknowledging every elimination that I was aware of (even if I couldn't get him to a potty on time), and practicing EC whenever I could without stressing out when I couldn't. The key is to focus on communication; the actual act of "catching" is less important than communicating and acknowledging what your child is doing. I often suggest to people just to try it for a half-hour each day; let your baby go bare-bottomed while lying on a soft waterproof pad or some cloth diapers. Or try putting your baby on the potty before bath time and make it a fun ritual. Even carried out part-time, EC makes for a beautiful bonding experience.

9. "We live in a city" or "We're always on the go."

Being an urban EC'er has its challenges, of course, but it's easier in other ways as well. You just have to adjust your thinking. It's not a big deal to pop a little lightweight plastic bowl in your diaper bag; after all, there's plenty of room if you're not using as many diapers. Also, just as a parent might loosely plan the day around feeding or nap schedules, once you're aware of your baby's elimination patterns you will develop an awareness of the optimal times for your outings. Many parents also find that they just rely on diapers more when life gets hectic or when they're going out, and that's totally fine too.

10. "I've decided to try it, and it's just not working—we have so many misses. I'm just not in tune with my baby."

Elimination communication used to be practiced throughout every society, and being surrounded by support and guidance was a given. It's just not as common today. This is why seeking out support— whether online, through a local DiaperFreeBaby support group, or by reading this book—is essential to success. Feeling discouraged from time to time is as common among EC'ers as it is among parents of older kids who are being conventionally toilet trained. Throughout the book, for each developmental stage, I will discuss how to approach the times when you feel out of sync with your child.

ABOUT THIS BOOK

Each chapter in this book will discuss a specific stage of development pertaining to EC. Although every chapter contributes to an overall sense of what EC is about and how it works for babies and young toddlers, if, for instance, you have a six-month-old and are reading this book for the first time, you may certainly skip directly to the chapter on mid-infancy. I'll repeat some of the most crucial information—how to cue, what your child's signals are, the logistics of doing EC at nighttime or on the go, etc.—to help you make sense of new issues that may arise as your child gets older. (For instance, you'll find that applying EC on the go with a newborn is different from practicing it with a walking, talking toddler. Each chapter will take into account your child's developmental stage.)

In the next chapter, "Gathering Support and Making the Leap," I briefly discuss some of the obstacles you might encounter as you prepare to practice EC with your baby. Just picking up this book is a wonderful sign that you are open to the possibilities of this method. Nevertheless, EC is so counter to the potty training dogma of the last several decades that you may find you need a bit more convincing to actually make the leap to practice EC. On the other hand, you yourself may be enthusiastic to get started, but you may have to convince a skeptical partner, relative, caregiver, or friend of the merits of this method. Take it from me; we've all been there, and this chapter will bolster your resolve.

In chapter 3, "Getting Ready to EC: Gear and Other Fun Stuff," you'll learn all about EC'ers' favorite items to help make infant pottying go smoothly. There is special clothing such as split-crotch pants, wool leggings to keep little legs cozy, and baby-sized training pants and underwear. I will introduce you to soft waterproof pads to spread out under your diaper-free baby when she's playing or sleeping, special potties just the perfect size for your infant, and other equipment that helps when you're out and about. I also discuss, in some detail, baby carriers and cloth diapers. You don't have to use either, but many parents do find them useful. Carrying your baby close to your body, especially at the start, helps you learn his elimination patterns. Coverless cloth diapers used on occasion can aid in providing a measure of "diaper-free" time for your baby, helping her retain her awareness of when she is going to the bathroom.

In chapter 4, "Newborn Bliss: Getting to Know Your Baby, Getting Started on EC," I'll focus on babies aged birth to three months and discuss how to connect with your newborn baby. I'll tell you how to get started, cover the typical experiences many parents go through, and teach you all the best EC'ing positions for a newborn.

You'll hear many parents' strategies for balancing life with a newborn while helping to address your baby's elimination needs.

In chapter 5, "EC'ing During Middle Infancy: Smooth Sailing," we're going to look at EC'ing a baby who is in middle infancy, which roughly covers ages three to eight months, or until baby really starts to become mobile. Whether you're just starting out or continuing on from the newborn stage, you'll learn about the basics of EC'ing during middle infancy. These babies are able to hold their heads up and sit on their own, which makes this a smooth and predictable time as babies' patterns become clearer and they are much more responsive and communicative. We'll talk about learning to read your baby's signals and introducing the potty or toilet. And of course there's plenty of information on EC'ing at night, on the go, or while working out of the home.

Chapter 6, "The Joys of EC'ing Your Mobile Baby," discusses EC'ing an older baby (roughly eight to twelve months) who is mobile and crawling, maybe even starting to walk and talk. You'll encounter new challenges at this time, whether you're continuing on or just getting started. Your baby is so excited by all his new developmental changes that he may be more distracted, but learning to walk and talk also introduces exciting opportunities for your child to take even more initiative with EC. Parents will tell you their strategies for keeping things going in a low-key, supportive, and loving way.

If you've got a one-year-old, you'll find chapter 7, "EC'ing Your Toddler," full of information you can use. It's so much fun at this age—your child is enthusiastic, loves to imitate adults, and is generally not going to be resistant in the way an older child might be. Whether you're just starting now or are continuing on from before, I'll discuss how to understand and work with your child, and how to lovingly keep him on the EC track even when he is so immersed in exploring and playing that he doesn't want to stop to go to the bathroom. You'll read lots of strategies for helping your child become more toilet-independent and involved in his own success.

Chapter 8, "Final Hurdles and Graduation," shows you how

many different families have dealt creatively with challenges such as toddler potty pauses as they approached "graduation," or toilet independence.

In the last chapter, "If Your Situation Is a Little Different," you'll hear from parents of preterm babies, multiples, and babies with special needs, whose unique situations might not have been covered in the previous chapters. I'll also briefly discuss how the gentle principles of EC can be adapted to aid toilet training a child of any age, including children older than eighteen months.

2.

Gathering Support and Making the Leap

So you've heard about infants using the potty and think it's a really interesting idea, but you're not completely sure it's for you. You're not alone. I've met many parents who heard about EC just once, perhaps from a friend or through a magazine or newspaper article, and instantly decided this was something that they wanted to try; it simply resonated with them. For every parent who is this enthusiastic and certain from the start, however, there is another who is intrigued but hesitant to make the leap.

Feeling reluctant is a very understandable reaction. After all, we are surrounded by dictates not to "rush" or "pressure" our children, and are told not to even consider introducing our children to the toilet until they are much older. We even have the luxury of purchasing large-sized disposable diapers so that our children can take all the time in the world to potty train. Although these cultural messages may lead us to fear making a mistake unless we follow standard toilet training rules to the letter, they are actually teaching us to ignore our own child's natural timetable. (You may recall, even when my older son's readiness was positively staring me in the face, I still hesitated because I had absorbed the cultural message that he was far too young by our society's standards.) Still others simply may not believe it is something a baby is even physically capable of, or they simply can't comprehend how the mechanism of EC works with a young, preverbal baby.

The very first thing to remember about EC, and something you'll hear me mention a lot, is that it is not about *toilet training* in the most commonly held view of the term. The reason many parents who practice EC dislike the word *training* in association with what they do is that this term has connotations that lead us away from the core of EC. EC is about communication, about gently getting in harmony with your baby, and proceeding at a pace that feels right for all of you. It's about engaging in a give-and-take on a daily basis and honing those instincts (the same instincts that allow you to sense when your baby is hungry, tired, or overstimulated) that make parenting your own unique baby so rewarding. There's nothing coercive, forced, or pressured about EC. You're not involved in a power struggle with a toddler or preschooler who is firmly attached to her diaper. It's not a race to get your baby out of diapers by a certain age. There are no expectations, except that you remain open to what your little one is saying to you. Most of all, it's about learning and following your baby's instinctive readiness signals—the ones she was born with.

Some parents may feel convinced that EC is good for parent and baby but are unable to imagine adding any further complications to their already-busy lives with an infant. In particular, the term *diaper-free baby* can be misleading to some people. I've met parents who were hesitant to embark on EC because they thought that this required their child to actually be completely free of diapers, and they couldn't fathom the kind of extra work this might take. I'm always quick to reassure them that being "diaper-free" has a much broader meaning than just going diaperless. Sure, many EC'ing parents find that they naturally evolve toward a stage where having their young baby or toddler in underwear or training pants rather than in diapers makes more sense; they may be very much in tune and having few

misses, or they may simply find that going diaper-free really facili-
tates the communication that is the cornerstone of EC. This is, however, not at all a prerequisite in any way. I really like how I've heard
some experienced EC'ing parents define what "diaper-free" means
to them: freedom from an exclusive reliance on diapers. It's simply
about knowing that you are not bound to diapers and that choosing
to exclusively diaper your baby is not an inevitable part of parenting
a new baby. If you choose to go diaper-free, it means you are making
a choice about how much you wish to be dependent upon diapers.
You're following an easy rhythm that you and your baby establish between yourselves. This may mean that you go through some phases
when you use many diapers a day, and others when you use very few
if any of them. There's certainly no expectation or requirement to be
diaperless all the time.

Some parents simply may not believe that EC is possible or they
may not understand how it works. Everything we as a society have
been taught in the last few decades by doctors, books, and even the
disposable-diaper industry would certainly lead many parents to believe that babies have absolutely no sphincter control or awareness of
elimination, and that minimal control doesn't even kick in until they
are well past infancy. Even if you believe that babies are physically
capable of some control over their elimination (and even if their instinctive desire not to soil themselves makes sense to you), the
process by which parent and child get in sync through nonverbal
cues, body language, and intuition might seem incomprehensible. If
you find yourself having these sorts of doubts, it may help to seek out
an EC'ing parent or DiaperFreeBaby group near you. There's nothing like an actual demonstration to show you how it all comes together. I've had nothing but positive, interested reactions from
people who have happened to witness my own babies being EC'ed.
In truth, seeing EC in action has a greater impact than just hearing
or reading about it.

If you find you are interested and nearly convinced but still teetering on the edge, I think the solution is simple. Just give it a try and see where it takes you. There's absolutely nothing to lose. Keep telling yourself that you'll try just one time, and then one more time after that, and recognize that you can stop anytime you want to. Before long, I predict you'll be hooked! Here are some stories from other EC'ing parents about how they got involved with EC.

I originally heard about EC from a friend. During a long international flight she met a young woman who was traveling with a young toddler after visiting India for several months. My friend was fascinated because the child was not wearing a diaper and told her mother when she needed to go to the bathroom—especially impressive, since both the child and mother had a stomach bug and the child had diarrhea. I remember thinking, "That's so crazy. You can't do that. I know, since it's already so hard to get my stepson to use the potty." Fast-forward to my being pregnant with my first child and we're *still* trying to potty train my stepson. While researching cloth diapers on the Internet, I stumbled across mention of EC and was hooked. It simply resonated with me this time. My friend still reminds me that she was the first one to tell me about this "wacky" idea!

—SAM, MOM TO WILLOW, 14 MONTHS

I heard of EC through a good friend. It seemed like an amazing idea, and at our first DiaperFreeBaby meeting she had my then two-month-old son take off his diaper in her house. He used the potty four times in a row without a miss. Needless to say, we never looked back.

—RIKKI, MOM TO DEXTER, 11 MONTHS

When I first heard about EC it seemed to counter many of the child development theories I'd heard, so I dismissed it. But when it came up again, I thought about it some more and realized it was probably the exact technique my grandmother used to train her three daughters. She always said they were potty trained by one year old, no fuss, and no muss. She also said, "If you know your child has to go, why would you make him go in his pants?" And that's how I've explained it to my parents. At first they laughed at another "crunchy" idea, but now they advocate it as common sense! They don't call it EC or infant potty training, but simply view it as a way for him to not go in his pants unnecessarily.

We're due with our first child in June and are looking forward to giving our baby a more comfortable relationship with bathroom habits. When I see his "potty face," I'll have no problem not making him go in his pants!

—MORIA, 8 MONTHS PREGNANT WITH FIRST CHILD

When I found out I was pregnant, my husband and I had lots of discussions about what we wanted for our baby. Since my husband is from India, I explained to him that although they used cloth diapers in his country, we would be using disposables, and he'd need to explain that to his mom when she came to help us out.

"No," he said, "I don't think we used cloth diapers with my little sister."

"Really," I asked, "you guys had disposables in the '80s?"

"No," he said, "I don't remember that, either."

The conversation—which was getting annoying—stopped there. Rachan can't ever remember his childhood, anyway, I thought, I am sure they used cloth. That was the end of it until my ninth month when Rachan was browsing the Web and found the DiaperFreeBaby site. "This is it!" he said, grabbing me away from my book. "We didn't use diapers. This is what my mom did. I can still hear her voice saying 'shhh pssst shhhh pssst' to my little sister."

He was over the moon about the EC movement in the United States; I, however, was committed to disposable diapers. I ruled out/laughed off EC, and once again, the conversation stopped there.

When we got home from the hospital it was disposable diapers all the way. But about a week after the baby was born, I was awoken from a nap to the sound of my mother-in-law saying "Shhh pssst shhhh psssst." I knew instantly what it was—and thought of the smile on Rachan's face when he recalled it.

We never discussed disposables, cloth diapers, or EC; it just happened. My mother-in-law started taking Jesse to the bathroom. I noticed we were saving lots on diapers. In fact, he grew out of the newborn size before we could finish the first pack. I realized that he was happy—noticeably happy—when he would pee or poop in the potty. On the other hand, he was unhappy—noticeably unhappy—sitting in a wet or dirty diaper for even a minute (uh, who wouldn't be?).

Like every mom, I wanted what was best for my son, and it was clear to me in every way that given the option, EC was his first choice. So, while it doesn't happen often, I'll admit this time I was wrong and my husband was right. EC saves us money, keeps our baby clean, and best of all, makes our special boy very, very happy.

—ANGELA, MOM TO JESSE, 15 MONTHS

GOING AGAINST THE TIDE: GETTING SUPPORT FROM OTHERS

Although you may be convinced and excited to practice EC, it's common to face skepticism from others. There will be times when it feels like every aspect of your parenting is up for public scrutiny and discussion. Toileting your child—no matter what his age—is no exception.

You may actually be surprised, however, at who does support

you. Many EC'ers report that their extended family members are very enthusiastic. Many proud grandparents are excited about what their grandchildren can do! And many parents who raised their children in a previous generation might actually be less resistant to the concept of an infant using a potty because this was not entirely unknown some decades ago. Remember, in my case, it was actually my own mother who first bought a potty for my barely-one-year-old. Other EC'ers I know report the same phenomenon: their mothers or grandmothers are the first ones to suggest putting their babies on the potty when they notice that the babies are going to the bathroom.

It can be a bit trickier when EC comes up with friends or relatives who also have young children, especially if they have made different parenting choices. Breast versus bottle, crib sleeping versus co-sleeping, and working versus staying at home all have the unfortunate potential to feel like divisive, even explosive, choices, and EC versus conventional toilet training is no different.

First of all, although it may feel difficult, try to be diplomatically firm about which family choices you are or are not willing to discuss. It's helpful to begin by showing your appreciation for the love and concern that the person you're addressing has for you and your child. This acknowledgment may help him or her remain open-minded when you explain that you have thought things through carefully and have made good decisions about what is best for your own family. Setting this boundary can help preempt uncomfortable conversations, if the topic even comes up at all. I recall one woman who came to our local group, relieved to "come out of the closet." She had always hidden the potties in her house whenever guests were over so they wouldn't question why she had potties for such a young infant!

Even if you remain private about EC, it's inevitable that at some point, someone is going to notice that you are taking your baby to the bathroom for something other than a diaper change. There are many misconceptions about EC. Some people might wonder aloud if it is coercive for the baby. Others may feel defensive about their own choices, or sad if they realize that their babies have been trying to communicate with them and they haven't noticed. It's also very common for people to feel indignant about EC because they see it as a throwback to a time when women in particular had fewer choices and led labor-intensive lives. EC is erroneously envisioned as being utterly overwhelming for the parent.

So what can you say in response to genuine but concerned queries about EC?

I've found that nearly everyone gains a different perspective on the practice when they realize it's simply another viable option for dealing with elimination. People are often receptive when I mention that exclusively diapered babies have actually been trained to go in their diapers. I often point out that many newborns will pee when their diapers are off, only to stop doing so as they become conditioned to go only in a diaper. (Some babies will even wait and go to the bathroom as soon as they're changed into a fresh diaper!) Parents who diaper their babies full-time are training their babies to use the diaper for their toileting needs, a habit parents will have to "unteach" a few years down the road. (And, of course, that option suits a lot of parents and children just fine.) But practicing EC even part-time or occasionally means your baby will not be exclusively diapered, and this has many great benefits. Such a realization helps people understand that full-time diapering is not the only choice they have.

Many parents I've spoken to also feel that there's actually little difference between the labor involved in EC and the labor involved in exclusive diapering, especially when you factor in the hard work that exclusive diaperers face when working with their older, diaper-reliant children. Parents practice EC in ways that fit their family situations, and for many families, this means some degree of part-time EC (even the full-time EC category has a built-in degree of part-time EC). Part-time or occasional EC—as little as one opportunity a day or less—takes very little time. Dressing your baby in easy-access clothing during the times you are at home and able to practice EC will make it even more convenient.

Sometimes actions speak louder than words. Because EC is carried out in such a natural, gentle, supportive way, people who have the chance to spend some time with you and your child will quickly see that this is not a coercive training program but rather a great way to follow your baby's cues and natural biological development. Thus your critics will probably become quite supportive of you. At the very least they are likely to recognize and respect the choice that you have made for you and your family.

> When we first started practicing EC, one of my friends said, "Oh, that sounds like training the parents," and my response was, "Well, yeah, just as much as learning to feed her when she's hungry."
>
> —KATE, MOM TO LUCIA, 6 MONTHS

> I was a closet EC'er for a long while. My parents and close friends knew we were doing it, but they sort of snickered and rolled their eyes about it. I didn't tell the moms at our playgroup until a conversation about infant potty training came up with a lot of misconceptions being thrown around. I couldn't *not* say anything, and by then we were pretty confident about our decision and choice to EC.
>
> —GIGI, MOM TO BEN, 18 MONTHS

> I can't recommend EC enough. Our own personal experience with EC has been so positive, gentle, and wonderful. Much like breast-feeding, after the initial learning period, we found EC to be a very laid back, enjoyable, gentle, and child-led process. Many folks think EC is a ton of extra work, but really it's not; it's a simple redistribution of the work that our culture currently puts into diapering for two-plus years, and then potty training.
>
> —MEGAN, MOM TO NOEMI, 30 MONTHS

When I tell people what we're doing, they mostly get hung up on how much work this must be. I'm not going to pretend that it isn't time-consuming, but so is any other aspect of childrearing. I prefer to hang out and play with toys with Ben while he goes in his potty rather than clean his diapers every day after wrestling him down to let me change them.

—SARABETH, MOM TO BEN, 8 MONTHS

Many times, people comment that time spent pottying an infant could be better spent playing. Having conventionally trained my first three kids, and having had a miserable time with it filled with frustration and anger on both sides, I can see how one might think that there must be a better way to spend time with one's child. It's different this time, EC'ing our baby. One of the things that I love most about EC is that potty time is fun. I sing to Eden, her siblings sing to her, and we smile at each other.

—BETH, MOM TO ZEV, 9, ARAVA, 6,
TEMIMA, 3, AND EDEN, 3 MONTHS

At first everyone thought I was crazy. But then I sent a book along with a baby potty to my sister, who had a little boy three months after I did. She thought it was strange, but gave it a shot, and the rest is history. Her son is an expert EC'er now, too! All it took to persuade the rest of our family and friends was a demonstration. Dexter is an adorable little ham, so he convinces everyone quickly.

—RIKKI, MOM TO DEXTER, 11 MONTHS

I noticed that the reactions I got from others changed as I myself got more comfortable and confident in what I was doing. At the beginning, I was skeptical of my own ability to practice EC. It also felt like the reactions I got from others were critical and filled with skepticism. I tried to remember that their comments were usually reactions to the choices they themselves had made. As I gained more confidence, I felt like any comments I received were now from people who were curious about EC and wanted to learn more.

—MARIE, MOM TO AIDAN, 29 MONTHS

My situation was a little different. My mother, who is from Ukraine, was more than supportive. It was summer when they visited and it was quite hot, so they didn't want to keep Yunna in a disposable when they took her on walks. My mom suggested that we buy Yunna some panties and just change them if she peed. When I told her that there is no underwear sold for babies so tiny, she simply could not believe it! She told me that I probably went to the wrong store and insisted on going with me to several children's stores to see for herself. She simply could not believe that babies in this country were kept in diapers for so long that the smallest underwear size was 2T!

—JULIA, MOM TO YUNNA, 11 MONTHS

SKEPTICISM CLOSER TO HOME

The larger problem that EC'ers may face is resistance within their own homes. Many parents run into a difference of opinion with their co-parent about whether to apply EC and to what degree. Many couples have differing degrees of tolerance for possible messes in the house, for instance, or different preferences for how they wish to spend their time with the baby. I admit that my own husband was very skeptical at first when he heard about EC. He wondered if this meant we'd have pee all over the house: a common concern.

If your partner is resistant for these reasons, point out that when you follow EC, a lot of waste ends up in the toilet instead of wadded up in the trash or smeared on a baby's body. Remind your co-parent that this is something you can practice very infrequently, and that he or she can help support the EC relationship in other ways (by helping to clean out the potties, for example) if he or she chooses not to practice EC directly. Often just getting started and letting your skeptical partner watch you practice EC will win him or her over in due time, especially when it's evident that baby is happily responding to the process.

Some parents may be willing to follow EC but feel as if they are not practicing it as well as their partners are. Again, this isn't uncommon. One partner often takes more of the lead in EC, and as a result, the other partner might feel less confident. Encourage your partner to form his or her own EC relationship with your child. Although you may rely on cues, your partner may use timing, or vice versa. I have a friend, Kate, whose husband never pottied their newborn, Lucia. One day Kate had positioned Lucia on the potty but had to leave for a second, so she told her husband, "Hold her here! Just go *pssss* till she pees," and left him with Lucia. After just a few more instances in which she asked her husband to take Lucia's diapers off and put her on the potty, he no longer needed instructions! Like Kate, guide your partner and then step back. Your child will also help to lead the way.

> When we first began EC, I managed to catch a few pees. My husband said, "Oh good, you just saved three diapers!" But at that point, he still wasn't really sure why he should help with this. Now he understands, has more confidence, and practices EC when he can.
>
> —ILANA, MOM TO LIAM, 11 MONTHS

> My husband participated from the beginning. I had to explain EC and model it for him, but once he had his first catch, he sure preferred practicing EC to changing a diaper!
>
> —LISA, MOM TO KAI, 3, AND NOE, 2

I wanted to try EC out of curiosity. My wife and I spent a lot of time traveling in Southeast Asia and India and we never saw kids in diapers. When Leslie got pregnant, I would tell her, "You know I don't believe in diapers; I'm not putting him in diapers." I was just joking, but she would get upset and say, "I don't want pee all over the house." Shortly before our son was born, I read an article about EC. It confirmed my theory that if you don't get a kid used to a diaper, he figures everything out much quicker. I was committed to finding out more, so I bought a book on EC. I realized it was much more about a philosophy of communication than a specific technique. This is what really sold me. I asked my wife to read part of the book, and she was also convinced. But when we began practicing EC, I was still taking the lead.

—KEVIN, DAD TO KAYDEN, 3 MONTHS

I was the one who was more gung ho about EC at first. It was difficult. My partner, Randi, got upset every time I took Rowan to the bathroom, especially if he fussed a bit. But I persisted, and within a few weeks Rowan became visibly excited whenever I took him to the bathroom, and quite happy when I caught a pee. That's what convinced Randi to keep going.

—CHARLES, DAD TO ROWAN, 8 MONTHS

My husband was a little skeptical when I started telling him about EC, but he remained open-minded and receptive. He is enthusiastic now because of how empowered our baby is to stay in a dry diaper and to communicate with us. My husband is also better than I am at picking up clear signals and cueing our boy to pee. Since my husband doesn't get to nurse, I think EC is a great bonding opportunity for them.

—EMILY, MOM TO OSCAR, 6 MONTHS

Many EC'ing couples who both work outside the home have also had great success getting their caregivers on board with EC. When looking for a nanny, some parents include EC in the interview process or seek out caregivers who come from cultures where EC is a mainstream practice. Others do not have such high expectations at the beginning but still find that, with time, their caregivers are receptive to trying EC. Caregivers can be just as intuitive and connected as parents. Some caregivers even experience what EC'ers call "phantom pees," when you imagine you've been peed on but it hasn't really happened—a sign that baby probably needs to pee.

Of course, if your caregiver remains resistant, you can still practice EC part-time during the times you yourself are home with the baby.

> My caregiver had never heard that babies could do this, but she found the idea fascinating. She's been practicing EC with Oscar and has been amazed at how he gives signals and goes on cue. She has been very successful with him. The first time she had a catch, I asked her how she knew he needed to go. She couldn't really explain what the intuition was based on but said that once she was looking for the signal, it was very clear.
>
> —EMILY, MOM TO OSCAR, 6 MONTHS

> Our fifteen-year-old babysitter was holding Helen in the kitchen. She suddenly looked confused and started checking herself because she said she felt as if she'd just been peed on. I explained that it was a "phantom pee" and is fairly common among some EC'ing folks. She looked at me like I was crazy, but after taking Helen to the bathroom, she came back saying, "I hate to say it, but you were right." She has been totally miss-free with Helen since learning about phantom pees!
>
> —KEILA, MOM TO JANE, 27 MONTHS,
> AND HELEN, 8 MONTHS

INSPIRATION: WHY PARENTS CHOOSE EC

If you're in need of a little more inspiration, here is some insight from EC'ing parents on why they decided to practice EC with their newborns.

For me, EC started to make sense after I read about the bonding and communication aspects. Waking up every morning and carrying Rowan off to the potty has become an integral part of our relationship, and his smile when I ask him if he wants to go to the potty is simply amazing. Using the bathroom is not a mystery to him; it's simply something that he knows how to do. This gives both of us a great sense of daily satisfaction. It's also really nice that with all of the things that are so "mom"—nursing, major comfort, and bonding—there is this one very important part of life that is "papa."

—CHARLES, DAD TO ROWAN, 8 MONTHS

EC is amazingly similar to breastfeeding on cue; you're just dealing with the other end of the feeding equation and looking for elimination signals versus hunger signals. The process becomes second nature to the point that you don't really think about it. You start to notice your baby's cues in the same way that you notice she is hungry without having to hover over her every minute.

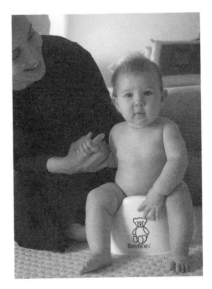

—MEGAN, MOM TO
NOEMI, 30 MONTHS

**EC provides many opportunities
to bond with your baby**

Although I know non-EC'ers take exception to this, I believe Simon and I have a closer connection because of our early and continuous interactions about his elimination needs. We never engaged in a diaper-changing struggle like so many parents do, nor did we have any toilet-training struggle. In addition, we were always dealing with his elimination in "real time" rather than after the fact, which I think makes a lot more sense to a baby.

—RACHEL, MOM TO ISAIAH, 6, AND SIMON, 3

I read about EC in a newspaper article, and my first thought was that it made sense. As a new mom, I am always trying to understand and care for my baby in every way possible. Why wouldn't I take care of her elimination needs as well? My main reason for trying EC was that I thought it would make my baby feel happy and more comfortable. That's what keeps me going. It's easier to be her mom if I can help her go.

—AMYLYNNE, MOM TO MEREDITH, 4 MONTHS

The environmental issue is big for me; it's a major concern that twenty-two billion disposable diapers are dumped into landfills annually. Doing what we can to minimize the impact of this waste is hugely appealing. Also, from what I hear about toilet training, EC is a much smoother and easier process and greatly reduces the strain on our baby. I like that he's more comfortable now not having to sit in a wet diaper.

—ERIK, DAD TO XANDER, 3 MONTHS

I had heard about EC but kind of ignored it until I noticed that my baby was very vocal about being wet. It was the number one thing that upset her. I had been hesitant about trying EC at first because I thought I'd have to do it full-time, but then I realized any little bit helps. Practicing EC halfway isn't really doing it halfway, if that makes sense. Having that knowledge gave me the permission to try.

—KATE, MOM TO LUCIA, 6 MONTHS

It's really easy to practice EC part-time. Once you open your mind to the idea that your baby is communicating with you about elimination, it's very easy to pick up his messages. It's obvious that it's on his mind and that he's telling you about it. And once you acknowledge that your baby prefers diaperless hygiene, you can't in good conscience ignore his cues.

—EMILY, MOM TO OSCAR, 6 MONTHS

Although I've EC'ed my own child, I do have experience with conventional potty training. I used to be an early childhood special education teacher and worked in several programs that had three- to five-year-olds with and without special needs. Many of the children, whether or not they had special needs, were yet to be potty trained. I remember feeling so sad for kids who were so attached to their diapers and so stressed by relearning where to go to the bathroom that I vowed to introduce my future children to the potty as early as possible.

—GIGI, MOM TO BEN, 18 MONTHS

3.

Getting Ready to EC: Gear and Other Fun Stuff

Just as a diaper genie, wipes warmer, diaper bag, and changing table can make conventional diapering easier, EC-friendly objects make EC a smoother experience overall. And with interest in EC so high, there is such a variety of helpful gear available that a newcomer could feel quite overwhelmed without a little introduction to what's out there. Read on to learn what EC'ers find useful, including potties, cloth training pants, cloth diapers, fleece pads for nighttime, and special clothes for EC'ed babies.

SLINGS AND BABY CARRIERS

You may be wondering what a discussion of slings and other baby carriers is doing in a book about elimination communication. The fact is, a lot of EC'ers also practice babywearing. I've been to many gatherings where I wasn't sure if I was at an EC or baby-wearing meeting! This is no mere coincidence. Many EC'ers like to keep their babies in a loving adult's arms much of the time, especially when they are so young and not yet mobile. You definitely don't have to do things this way—EC is perfectly doable even if your baby isn't constantly in your arms—but lots of new parents are thrilled to learn about anything that makes it easier for babies to stay snuggled close for the brief period they are so small. Let me explain further why you might want to consider looking into the wonderful variety of baby carriers out there and how they aid EC in particular.

EC, especially during the newborn and middle-infancy stages, is much easier when you have a baby that is in close proximity to you. In most of the cultures where EC is still commonly practiced society-wide, babies are almost constantly in-arms. Because of this, their parents are so attuned to every little squirm that they can quickly tell when their baby has to go to the bathroom.

It is also important to note that babies generally prefer to be off your body and out of a sling when eliminating. When you do take your baby out of a sling, you have a natural opportunity to potty him because he's likely not to go while he is in your arms. You and baby will get used to each other's rhythms—it's not as if keeping him in a sling is going to force him to hold it in. He's probably going to be in a nice state of "quiet alertness" or sleep while in the sling, which indicates that he's comfortable and doesn't need to go to the bathroom. If he starts to squirm or fuss or show other signs of needing to go, you'll be right there to take him out of the carrier, put him in the right position, and help him. Also, depending on the kind of carrier you use, your small baby can be diaper-free while he is on your body. You can just pad the carrier with a light layer of cloth, like a flat cloth diaper, and let baby be skin-to-skin with you, enhancing this special bonding time with your baby while remaining aware of his elimination patterns.

Parents Speak about Babywearing and EC:

Using a sling allowed us to carry Felix with our hands free and kept us physically in touch with him, which made his signals far easier to pick up. We also quickly discovered that Felix would not eliminate while being carried in the wrap or while sleeping in it. This made EC'ing while out and about a snap. We'd toilet him before leaving, pop him into the wrap at our destination, and take him out to toilet when he woke or signaled (usually by fussing or squirming in the wrap).

—KAREN AND PRAVEEN,
PARENTS TO FELIX, 17 MONTHS

WHAT KIND OF CARRIER IS BEST FOR ME?

I was a real baby-wearing addict when my first son, Benjamin, was born, and I experimented with pretty much every type of baby carrier out there. My favorites were a simple padded ring sling for its ease of use, a soft backpack carrier because it felt so comfortable to wear the baby on my back, and, when he was a bit older, a hip carrier or pouch just to provide a little extra support when he was hoisted onto my hip. Sometimes I used a long wrap that I wound around my body in certain ways to form a pouch for the baby on my front or back. I also used a Korean blanket back carrier called a "podeagi" because I had plenty of relatives around to teach me how to use it. In the end, I was so into babywearing, but so frustrated by the lack of good options out there, that I ended up buying reams and reams of fabric to try to design my own versions of baby carriers and slings—some successful, others less so!

The good news is that in the few years since then, the variety of baby carriers available has multiplied unbelievably as babywearing has become more popular. No need to make your own (unless you are so inclined). I can virtually guarantee that you are going to find something that suits your needs. Let me give you an overview of some of the basic types out there and how to use them.

Ring Slings

You've probably seen a ring sling; they've become popular in recent years. A ring sling is made of a long piece of fabric, which might or might not be padded. (This is a matter of personal preference. Generally, padded slings can be more comfortable but are also bulky, whereas unpadded slings are more adjustable but may not be as comfortable for some people. I really like having both types on hand.) One end of the sling is sewn to two rings, and the other, loose, end of the sling is threaded through the rings to make a large loop. The whole thing is put across your body over one shoulder, and you wear baby in the pocket formed by the sling itself. The beauty of this carrier is that it allows your baby to position himself in a variety of ways. He can be sitting up, lying down, facing in or out—whatever suits you and your baby best. It's also really quick and easy to use—you can just pop baby in and out of the sling with minimal effort. Because it's worn over only one shoulder, you can adjust the sling by pulling the material through the rings to provide a close fit for your baby and your body. Some slings are made in the ring-sling pro-

totype but are actually more like pouches because they use snaps or are sewn shut instead of using adjustable rings. They are available in a variety of fabrics, from plain old cotton to hemp, linen, mesh, fleece, and even gorgeous fabrics such as silk shantung.

A mother holding her baby in a ring sling. Babywearing helps EC'ers get in tune with their babies' elimination patterns.

Wrap Slings

Wrap slings are among the simplest carriers available. The sling consists of a long piece of fabric wound about your body in a variety of different ways. The fabric length is long so that it can be wound around the body several times. New parents might find this process daunting, but practice makes perfect. The versatility of these slings is priceless. You can wear baby on your front, back, or side, and baby is securely worn against your body. The wrap usually goes over both shoulders so that you get the benefit of multiple support points over the shoulders as well as on the hips. Babywearing feels much easier when you do it this way. Wrap slings have been used all over the world, in many different cultures. They are made of different materials; some people like the firm fabric of a Mexican rebozo, whereas others prefer wrap slings made of stretchier material. Wrap slings made of woven material, such as the Didymos and Storchenwiege, are popular and come in beautiful patterns. Wrap slings are also versatile because they can be used as blankets when needed. These are the easiest slings to make yourself if you are so inclined, as they are just long pieces of fabric.

Mei-Tais

A Mei-tai is a traditional Chinese-style baby carrier, and there are many variations of this prototype out there. The carrier is made of a square piece of cloth with four wide ties coming out from the corners. Baby is worn against the adult's body, either in front or on the back. As with wrap slings, there's a bit of a learning curve when first using mei-tais, but with practice it becomes completely effortless to wear your baby in this carrier. The snug fit and cross-shoulder straps greatly minimize back strain, enabling you to carry your baby for long periods of time.

Hip Carriers, Tube Slings, and Pouches

Once your baby is older and able to sit up, you may want to look into buying a hip carrier, tube sling, or pouch. These are similar to ring slings in that they go across one shoulder, but they are sleeker and made with minimal fabric. When positioned in one of these carriers, baby sits up perched on one of your hips. Hip carriers often come with a hip strap as well for additional support. Pouches and tube slings come in many different materials such as fleece, cotton, and even mesh so you can wear baby in the water. The Maya pouch and the hiphugger are just a few of the many popular choices out there.

Soft Backpack

Soft backpack carriers (which can also be used to carry baby in the front) are designed with strategically placed padding to minimize back, shoulder, and neck strain. Because they have some structure built in, they generally require less of a learning curve than back carriers with ties. I've found that these types of carriers are particularly favored by fathers. My favorite backpack carrier is the Ergo, which also has wide hip straps so that your baby's weight is resting on your hips. An Ergo backpack even makes carrying a heavy toddler seem easy.

Because your baby is growing so quickly, you may find that there isn't just one kind of carrier that suits all your needs. Some people prefer different carriers for different situations or for different stages of the baby's life. I liked having my baby on my back in a soft backpack carrier when I was moving in to a new home and unpacking, because the carrier needed very little readjusting and I could keep him on my back for a long time. On the other hand, I liked having him in a sling for walks or when we were on the go because I liked having his face so close in front of me. Having a small variety of carriers, or perhaps just a couple to keep handy here and there (like in the car, by the entranceway, etc.) is not a bad idea. Most baby-wearing fans definitely own more than one carrier!

QUICK TIPS: BABYWEARING

- Keeping baby close when starting EC helps you and baby become in sync with one another

- There are many different types of baby carriers out there: ring slings/pouches, wrap slings, mei-tais, tube slings and pouches, and soft backpacks

- Not all slings serve every purpose. You might benefit from having a couple on hand to use for different situations or to switch around as baby gets older and your needs change

- Baby usually will let you know when she needs to get down to go to the bathroom. Offer an opportunity to use the toilet when she is taken out of the sling

CLOTH DIAPERS: WHY THEY ARE USEFUL EVEN IF YOU ARE NOT USING CLOTH DIAPERS

Before I begin this section, let me be clear about one point: EC is completely achievable even if you use disposables the whole way through. I've met many parents whose babies exclusively wore disposables who have applied EC with great success. If you like the convenience of disposables, there is no need to worry that practicing EC means you have to switch over to cloth.

That said, let me share some reasons why having at least a few cloth diapers on hand can make EC smoother. And remember—like all other aspects of EC—it's certainly not an all-or-nothing situation. You can carry out EC with a combination of mostly disposables and an occasional cloth diaper, or switch to using more cloth (diapers and training pants) as you and your baby get more in harmony with each other and are having so few misses that it makes sense to switch out of expensive disposables. (I've met many parents who were full-time disposables users but decided to switch to a bit of cloth after starting EC. The amount of money they would save was highly compelling—especially since they'd frequently find themselves throwing out dry diapers.) You can also use cloth diapers full-time, either ones that you launder yourself or diapers delivered by a local diaper service. Remember, there are a number of options out there—do what feels right for your family.

If you're curious about cloth diapers but have always felt daunted by the thought of using them, I hope this little overview will reassure you that they're really not all that mysterious or complicated. And using some cloth at least part of the time does help EC for a couple of reasons. First of all, it's easier to connect with your baby quickly when you are able to immediately tell whether he has gone or not (and this is difficult to ascertain if he's in a disposable,

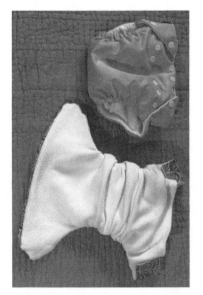

which is designed to feel dry even after a baby has peed in it). So if you are committed to trying EC once a day, you might consider using a cloth diaper during that time. Cloth diapers or training pants make for a nice transitional bridge; they are a good alternative to going totally diaper-free until

Cloth diapers with snaps or Velcro fastenings are as easy to use as disposables.

you and your baby are ready to take the plunge, or if you have a lot of carpet in the home and really don't feel your floors can accommodate a diaper-free environment.

Cloth Diapering Systems

As with baby carriers, there is such a huge variety of cloth diaper types available that it could make any parent's head swim. The following is a quick introduction to some basic types of cloth diapers. If this piques your interest, see the section at the end of the book for additional information on more specific diapering systems and diaper care.

Prefolds and Covers

Prefolds are little rectangular pieces of cotton or hemp fabric sewn together to make a thick layer of cloth. They're usually thicker in the middle than at the sides. You can buy them in different sizes and in different amounts of layers to meet your needs. When I was using cloth diapers before getting into EC, I bought the most absorbent prefolds I could find so that my baby could go longer without needing to be changed. Once we started EC'ing, however, I found it more useful for our purposes to have on hand the thinnest ones possible, enough to absorb just one pee.

The hands-down favorite among most cloth-diapering aficionados are Chinese or diaper-service quality (DSQ) prefolds. Their simple shape allows them to be used in a variety of ways. While some parents pin them on their babies, others simply fold and lay them inside a diaper cover, which can be made of polyester or nylon, cotton (treated to be water-repellent), fleece, or wool (which is one of the most naturally water-resistant fabrics out there). These covers are simple to use because most of them fasten with Velcro. Unless the cover is actually wet or dirty, it doesn't need to be washed after every single use—just air it out. It is common to rotate several covers for a while before washing them.

Thick prefolds are great for cloth diaperers, but experienced EC'ers find that they actually prefer thinner ones because, folded up appropriately, they are enough to absorb just one pee, make for less laundry, and dry more quickly. It's probably a good idea to have some of each—the thinner and the thicker prefolds—on hand to see what works best.

You can also purchase a prefold belt. This is a piece of fleece-wrapped elastic that goes around your baby's waist and can hold a prefold between her legs without your needing to use a cover. These are great for those times when you're hanging out at home.

I strongly recommend that you purchase a few prefolds, whether or not you're going to actually use them as cloth diapers. They are incredibly useful for the EC'ing family or any family with a young baby. You can tuck one inside a sling, lay one under your sleeping, diaper-free baby, or spread one out under your baby when he's sitting up but not mobile. They're also useful to have on hand to wipe up any messes that you might encounter. You can easily purchase a dozen good quality prefolds for little more than you'd pay for a big package of disposables. (One warning: most of the prefolds you see in a baby store are not the highly absorbent, good-quality kind. Avoid wasting your money on these. See resources on page 203 for a list of reputable cloth-diapering websites.)

Fitted Diapers

Fitted diapers are diapers that will stay on the baby even without a cover. They have gathers sewn at the legs and waist and they fasten either with snaps or Velcro fastenings. Think of them as thick, absorbent training pants that can be unfastened from the side like a disposable diaper. Being able to take them off in this way is useful if your baby has pooped inside the diaper and you need to take it off without pulling it down your baby's legs. The biggest advantage of fitted diapers is that they make a fabulous diaper–training pant for an EC'ed baby who is fairly reliable but is not yet in underwear or training pants. Of course, you can put a waterproof cover on top of the fitted diaper, but in general, a lot of EC'ing parents find that they keep their babies in these alone, especially when they are at home. You do have to be more specific about the size of fitted diapers than you do with prefolds. Fitted diapers need to fit your baby well, especially around the thighs, to be effective. Kissaluvs are one of many popular fitted diaper brands.

Pocket Diapers

One special type of diaper that I must make note of are pocket diapers; the best-known brand is Fuzzi Bunz. These are diapers made of a waterproof outer layer and a fleece inner lining with an absorbent insert (a prefold, a special insert made of microterry, or any rag or scrap of cloth will work!). When the baby pees, the fleece next to her skin wicks moisture away from her bottom, which makes these cloth diapers suitable for situations in which an immediate change is not always possible or for use as a backup or nighttime diaper. An additional benefit to using these diapers is that you can feel inside the pocket to check whether the baby has gone. One caveat: some parents I know feel that while fleece pocket diapers are very convenient, they are similar to disposables in how well they prevent baby from recognizing that she has gone to the bathroom. In an older baby, especially, this can impede awareness and communication between the two of you. You may want to consider increasing your vigilance during the times when your baby is wearing a pocket diaper (by loosely keeping track of timing or being more alert to your baby's cues), or else be sure to alternate use of pocket diapers with other forms of diapers or training pants.

All-in-Ones (AIOs)

My husband loves all-in-ones. He invested in a huge stash of Bumkins, the all-in-one diaper that we relied on the most. Why did he like these so much? He never really felt like he got the hang of laying a prefold in a diaper cover, but all-in-ones are so similar to disposables in their shape and convenience that he was quite enthusiastic about them. Basically, they are a flannel diaper and waterproof cover sewn together and fastened with Velcro straps at the sides. They can be put on or taken off your child in as little time as it would take to change a disposable. All-in-ones are pricier than other diapers. But if you invest in them once, you can use the same diapers for two or three babies (especially if those babies are being EC'ed part-time and aren't using the diapers all that much!). We invested a couple hundred dollars in all-in-ones ranging from newborn to toddler sizes, which we used for two children (and they are still good for another baby to use)—a far cry from the many thousands of dollars we would have spent on conventional diapering and toilet training two kids!

TRAINING PANTS AND TINY LITTLE UNDERWEAR

Once you and your baby are really in sync with each other and are having very few misses, it makes little sense to keep your baby in cloth diapers or costly disposables. Unfortunately, one of the biggest

Side snaps make training pants easy to take off a crawling baby.

challenges for EC'ing families has been finding pint-sized training pants and underwear. Luckily, a growing number of small companies are producing these goods for EC'ing families, and there's now a wonderful variety of products from which to choose. Many of the EC-oriented infant training pants available have a small layer of absorbent cotton cloth on the inside to absorb about one miss. They are similar to the fitted diapers described on pages 48 to 49 in that they have snaps on the sides so that they can be taken off easily without having to take baby's entire bottom layer of clothing off. However, training pants are much trimmer than fitted diapers. Many training pants, such as Poquito Pants and Snap Pants, have a water-resistant nylon or polyester layer on the outside and a soft cotton layer inside, against your baby's skin. Snap Pants, KISSes, and Poquitos are all available either waterproof or nonwaterproof. Other products, such as Bright Bots, may not have a water-resistant layer, but are basically training pants that are sized to fit an infant. There are also training pants and underwear available in pure organic cotton. These pants are thick enough to absorb just one pee, but this is the point of them; if you're EC'ing, you don't want something that will absorb pee after pee and leave your baby in the equivalent of a wet diaper. You can also find extra small underwear and training pants, although many families resort to buying size 2T underwear and shrinking them in a hot-water wash until they fit baby, more or

Bright Bots training pants

less. Hanna Andersson training pants and underwear are favored by many EC'ers for their high quality, fit, and durability, but there are several other suitable brands as well. Gerber training pants are another option; they are widely available and inexpensive. If you find you need a little extra protection, you can put a diaper cover over the training pant.

By the way, remember that if your baby is in underwear or training pants, her clothes are going to fit differently without a bulky diaper. You might have to keep a couple of smaller-size pants or leggings if you have an EC'ed baby. My son stayed in three-month-size pants from three months to nearly a year.

(See the resources section at the end of the book for purchasing information.)

EC CLOTHING

You EC'ing parents today don't know how lucky you are! When I was EC'ing my sons, I found myself making homemade adjustments to regular clothes, like opening the crotch seams in tiny leggings or buying knee-highs meant for an older child to keep my baby's legs warm while he was in a training pant at home. In just a few years, the number of special clothes available just for EC'ing families has grown tremendously. There is now a great variety of EC-friendly clothing out there.

A woman once asked at a DiaperFreeBaby meeting if practicing EC meant that her baby would never be able to wear normal clothes, like all those cute things you received at your baby shower. I'm here to say that's absolutely not the case! Don't worry—you will get use out of "regular" clothes. I know that dressing those tiny babies in cute clothes is part of the fun of having a baby (not that EC clothing isn't cute too, because it really is). But since getting your baby's clothes off quickly when she needs to use the potty is part of what makes EC'ing so achievable, it's worth looking into a

One Mom Speaks About Going Diaper-Free

There are many ways to start including cloth training pants or underwear in your diaper routine. It is so much fun to see your baby in trim EC undies! I might buy a few of each of the various kinds I find appealing and build up gradually until I have enough to make one laundry load. Depending on the day, I might

- decide to use training pants or underwear for a set period of time (four hours for example);

- use the entire stash until it's all used up, or

- decide to use a set number of training pants per day. Some people use, say, three pairs a day and then switch to diapers (either cloth or disposable) until the next morning.

Having a baby is an adventure in laundry, and doing diaper-type laundry doesn't need to be scary. With EC especially you may not need a diaper pail at all. Training pants and cloth diapers can easily be rinsed and then washed with regular laundry. I wash often and gently, using as little soap as possible, and avoid all softeners and detergent additives. These will only coat the fabric, making them less absorbent. Stains can usually be "sunned out"; just lay the material in a sunny spot after washing to dry.

I definitely noticed my daughter's change in attitude when she was in trimmer undies instead of diapers. She had more freedom of movement and seemed more comfortable. What's better than that?

—EMILY, MOM TO DELIA, 2

few items of EC clothing, even if just for occasional use when hanging out at home.

Split-crotch pants originated in China, where bare bottoms on babies and young kids are a common sight. They consist of leggings or pants that are open where the crotch seams usually are. The pants appear closed when baby is walking around, but open up when baby squats to go to the bathroom. Lots of EC'ing parents will put a split-crotch pant on their baby, especially when at home, and tuck a pre-fold diaper in there for a little extra padding in case baby has a miss. One business, The EC Store, carries woolen split-crotch leggings, which are a wonderful way to keep your baby warm in the winter while facilitating EC. I've also seen them sold in cotton, fleece, and even sumptuous velvet!

If you don't have any split-crotch pants, there are other options available. My friend Elizabeth actually finds a good use for the one-piece coveralls that are so popular. While I generally find that one-piece clothing can make EC more difficult, especially with a newborn, Elizabeth leaves some of the snaps open near the crotch, in effect making a "homemade" split-crotch outfit.

BabyLegs are little baby-sized leg warmers that cover the leg from ankle to thigh (kind of like a very long footless sock). Dressing your baby in just a top and a disposable or cloth diaper, training pant, or underwear, especially at times when you know she may need to use the potty more frequently, makes it much easier to help her to the bathroom without

Split-crotch pants

BabyLegs and other leg warmers help keep babies' and toddlers' legs warm while they're diaper-free.

much fuss. BabyLegs simply keep her little legs from becoming cold or her knees from getting scraped when crawling around. Another alternative to BabyLegs are knee-highs. I found cute striped knee-highs that fit my baby perfectly in the feet and went all the way up to the middle of his thigh. They didn't have non-skid padding, but you can easily put the padding on yourself if you've got a toddler who might slip while running around. And of course, keeping a little girl in a dress or even a boy in a longer tuniclike top are good ways to keep your baby dressed and warm while making quick EC pottying a snap.

WATERPROOF PADS

You should consider purchasing some sort of waterproof pad, like a large-sized lap pad or changing pad. Have several on hand around the house, as these are very useful for providing diaper-free time to your baby. In addition to changing or lap pads that you can get at any baby supply store, there are double-thickness fleece pads, which make a comfortable place for baby to lie down on, and PULpads, which are waterproof on one side and absorbent hemp on the other. I also loved having a large wool felt puddle pad around. It appealed to me because wool is a natural fiber that is naturally water-repellent and is easy to care for. You can spread a soft blanket on top of a wool pad and let baby lie on it. They are expensive, but they are so versatile and durable that you will find many uses for them. (Perhaps it will help you to justify the cost of this item and other EC gear if you remember that, on the whole, you are saving quite a bit of money by following EC.) Many parents lay a large pad underneath baby when he's having some tummy time or when he's sleeping; the pads are especially useful if your baby's diaper-free at night. Fleece or wool pads can also be used to help form a cozy playing spot for a baby who's sitting up—just scatter some toys around.

POTTIES AND POTTY COVERS

When your baby is a newborn, you will probably EC her either in your arms over a toilet, or into a small bowl in your lap. You can use any bowl or container that you find useful, but there is a specific, specially shaped bowl called a Potty Bowl available from The EC Store designed to fit right between your thighs, making it easy to position an EC baby when she is in your lap. The Potty Bowl also helps you EC discreetly, which many parents like. The bowl is small and light enough to pop into your diaper bag and take with you when you're on the go. My friend Melinda finds that an empty sour cream container fits perfectly in the bottom of the Potty Bowl, making cleanup even easier when you are out.

Soon, your baby will be able to sit on a real potty. For some babies, this could happen as early as two months of age. There are lots of potties out there, but the universal favorite of EC'ers is the Baby Bjorn Little Potty. It is small and low to the ground, and very, very stable. It comes in a variety of colors. There is also a clear potty, called the Babywunder Deluxe Clear Potty, sold by The EC Store, shaped exactly like a Baby Bjorn Little Potty. The advantage of this is that you don't have to lift your baby to see if she's gone to the bathroom, and you'll be able to cue her exactly when she's going!

You might also be interested in Potty Cozies and Potty Turtlenecks—fleece covers that fit on the rim of the potty bowl or the potty. These are especially helpful during cold weather or at night-time, when the feel of a cold plastic potty might startle your baby.

When your baby is ready to sit on a toilet with a toilet insert, again, you have many choices. Personally, I really liked the Baby Bjorn Toilet Trainer, which is a seat reducer that fits right on the toilet seat. This one is particularly nice if you have a boy because it has a raised rim in the front, but it's smooth and comfortable and obviously great for a girl too. There are many other good toilet reducers on the market as well.

When they're on the go, some parents report that they like to use a travel potty, such as the Potette On the Go Portable Potty. This potty comes with disposable liners that are designed to be small and portable enough to toss into a diaper bag.

By the way, none of these purchases are necessary to give EC a try. You can just hold your baby over a toilet or a plastic container from your kitchen, and you can use plain old washcloths or flannel squares instead of prefolds; that's really all it takes! But if you're in the swing of things, you're definitely going to find some of this gear useful. Now it's time to learn how to really start the exciting process of EC with your baby!

4.

Newborn Bliss: Getting to Know Your Baby, Getting Started on EC

Congratulations! You have a sweet little newborn baby. This is such an incredible time in your lives, as you and your little one begin to learn about each other for the first time. It can be a blissful time, but it can also feel overwhelming. Recovering from pregnancy and birth, getting off to a good nursing start, dealing with interrupted sleep, and incorporating your baby into your family if you already have other children can make this a joyful but tumultuous time.

Your first priority should be to get plenty of rest, eat well, get as much help as you can, and put your regular lives on hold for a bit as you embark on your "babymoon." Spend as much time as you can getting to know your new little baby.

Whenever you feel ready, however, you can start EC. Anytime during these first three months of life is ideal for you to begin because newborn babies still possess such a keen bodily awareness of elimination.

HOW TO BEGIN: OBSERVATION

If you are so inclined, beginning EC right at birth is not as difficult as one might think. It's always helpful to start EC by simply observing your baby's body language and her patterns, and this is a great time to do that. Also, babies have less output right at the beginning, aside from meconium. It actually makes sense, from a health perspective, to be as aware of your baby's elimination as you can during the few days after she is born. If you are breast-feeding your baby, the amount and frequency of your baby's output is an important indicator that she is nursing well. You can diaper your tiny newborn, lay her upon a blanket, towel, or open prefold, or simply keep her wrapped a bit more loosely with a coverless cloth diaper or loose disposable diaper between her legs. If your baby is a boy, you can place a small wash-cloth over his penis to prevent being sprayed. This makes it easy for you to check if baby has gone or not without disturbing her.

I also highly recommend that you avoid those one-piece romper-type clothes during the first few weeks, whether you are EC'ing or not. Newborns are sensitive to change, and having to change a baby from head to toe with each diaper change can disturb her. Dress baby in a separate top and bottom, or even a shirt or two on top with blankets or leggings to cover her bottom, to make it easier for her (and you!) during this time. Later on, when she is less sensitive to the newness of everything, you can use a wider variety of clothing.

Your baby is still developing patterns in every way, and her sleep and eating may be somewhat erratic in the first few weeks after birth. This means that elimination, too, is probably more erratic than it will be later on. Still, there are a few general rules of thumb to keep in mind. First of all, babies often eliminate upon waking and during or immediately after a feeding. These are good times for you to observe if your baby is going to the bathroom, to let her know that you're aware of what she is doing, or to actually offer her a chance to go. At this age, babies go more frequently, so the chances are high that your baby will actually go to the bathroom when you offer her a chance to go. Think of it this way: all that peeing and pooping that newborns are famous for means many more opportunities for you to connect with your baby!

HOW TO CUE

What is cueing, anyway? Cueing is an absolutely vital part of EC. When you cue your baby, you're holding her in a certain position while making a certain sound. Many parents instinctively make a sound like *"psssst,"* or some other shushing noise that sounds like water for cueing pees, but you can choose whatever sound comes most naturally to you. You can use the same noise for bowel movements, or you can choose a different sound. Many parents find themselves making a soft, modified grunting noise, imitating the baby herself going to the bathroom. For some reason, this tends to work for most babies. My friend Elizabeth also cues her baby to relax by exhaling on his head. If your baby is peeing while having a bowel movement (or if you think she's about to), you can alternate cues.

Interestingly, these cues in general are common across families and cultures. They feel very instinctive and babies respond to them. The more often that you make these cues while your baby is eliminating, the more she will associate the very position and sound with your taking her to the bathroom. Eventually she will release her bladder or bowels if they are full when you cue her. This communication is one of the cornerstones of EC'ing an infant.

If you happen to catch your baby in the act of going, such as when you take her diaper off (many newborns will immediately start to go then), simply cue her right away as she finishes. Repeated experiences cueing her while she is going will strengthen her associations among the sensation of going, the sound you make, and her position. It is particularly helpful during the newborn in-arms phase for you to hold your baby without actually fastening a diaper on her, especially at times you know she may be likely to go (such as after she wakes up or while nursing). If she is lying in your arms with a loose, unfastened disposable or cloth diaper underneath her bottom or tucked between her legs, you'll immediately be able to tell when she is going to the bathroom and can cue her by making the cue sound you've chosen.

Parents Speak About Starting to EC a Newborn:

On the day my baby Helen was born, she lay in my arms all day wrapped in a receiving blanket with prefolds under her bottom. The prefolds were loosely in place, and if I ever thought she needed to potty or if she were going, I'd cue her with a sound while trying to get comfortable holding her in a good position.

—KEILA, MOM TO JANE, 27 MONTHS,
AND HELEN, 8 MONTHS

We bought a few Tupperware bowls before she was born. Basically, we'd take her diaper off and put her over the pot right before a diaper change. We knew her patterns; she always pees right after she wakes up, so we often tried after naps.

—HEIDI, MOM TO RUBY,
5 WEEKS OLD

A two-week-old newborn held over a cloth diaper for an "observation" period. An open cloth or disposable diaper makes it easy to observe and quickly cue baby when she's going to the bathroom.

We started with both children from birth. EC'ing such a small baby is just pure fun. Anybody who holds such a tiny being and sees it relax and pee and smile will experience that.

—BIRGIT, MOM TO JOSCH, 4, AND NELLY, 2

POSITIONING A NEWBORN

I really like to encourage parents to start off small, although I completely applaud those of you who are motivated to do this throughout the day as often as you can. Any degree of EC is a really wonderful thing for your baby. There are many different ways you can do this, and you can experiment with what works for your family. You can decide on periods of diaper-free time here or there, or you can hold your baby over a Potty Bowl, container, or toilet after a diaper change or before a bath. There are many parents who only use EC for bowel movements because they are so obvious. In fact, a lot of parents I've met only catch bowel movements throughout infancy, deciding that they will approach pee training later in a more conventional way.

If you are feeling awkward carrying out EC or if you are still trying to get the hang of it, you can always leave your baby diaperless (or loosely diapered) for ten minutes after one of his diaper changes, say, once a day or so. Figure out what positions he is comfortable in. Not all babies will be comfortable at first in the typical newborn EC holds, but keep checking back every few weeks. A position that your baby is not comfortable in at one point in his development might become a favorite later on when he's older. By the same token, as his body changes and new abilities develop (such as the ability to hold his head up or to sit independently), he may outgrow his fondness for positions that might have been comfortable when he was younger. Be aware of these possibilities. Your baby may even have a preference for one position one day and another position the next. The one constant about babies is that they are constantly changing!

There are many positions you can use to EC a newborn, but one of the most common ones is the in-arms position over a toilet or even a sink (see photo). To do this over a toilet, you can squat in front of the bowl holding your diaper-free baby under her thighs. She will be completely enfolded in your arms so that she feels safe and comfortable. You can also straddle the toilet bowl yourself, facing backward, with baby in the same position. Baby can also be sideways and cradled in your arms while you do this, if she's small enough. You can start cueing her while she's in this position, repeating the *"psst"* sound, if it seems to you that she is probably due for a pee or poop.

It may also be very comfortable for your baby if you hold her in the in-arms position but do it over a bowl or a loose or open diaper. You can even position baby to pee in a Potty Bowl in your lap. This is an especially good position to try if you're nursing. Many young babies will eliminate while they are nursing, and their mothers find that by continuing to nurse them while leaving their bottoms bare, they can feed their babies at the same time that they are assisting them to go to the bathroom.

You can expect that it may not go smoothly right away. The key to EC is figuring out the right balance—remaining gently persistent while also recognizing when your baby is or isn't ready for a new position. Don't give up, even if it doesn't seem to work at first. Most

A two-week-old newborn held in the in-arms position over a toilet. Baby feels very secure in this position.

parents find that having a couple of different EC tricks in their tool-box allows them greater flexibility and a higher chance of success-fully finding positions that work well for their babies.

I really like how one mom I know, Amylynne, introduced herself and her baby to EC. For the first week, she would leave little Mered-ith in her diaper but just put her in position and cue and soothe her whenever she saw her straining. By the end of the week, her baby would automatically go when Amylynne put her in position and cued her. The baby would actually look to her mother to assist her. It was clear they'd both gotten the hang of what they were doing, so Amylynne was able to proceed to the next step: cueing her over a toilet without the diaper.

> At three months, Helen went through a phase in which she seemed to become uncomfortable using the potty. When she wouldn't go in that, I held her over the toilet and she went right away.
>
> —KEILA, MOM TO HELEN, 27 MONTHS,
> AND JANE, 8 MONTHS

IF YOU HAVE A MISS

EC'ers refer to pees and poops that they don't catch as "misses." Misses are a fact of life when practicing newborn EC. It's important to realize this and not feel discouraged or think you are doing some-thing wrong. It is part of the process of getting to know your child. Don't discount the success of noticing a pee right after she's gone. Even a miss can be thought of as a wonderful opportunity. You can reflect, look back, think about her behavior right before she peed, and store that information away: "I see that my baby squirms right before she needs to go to the bathroom," or, "My baby stops nursing right before a poop," and so on. Every time your baby pees or has a bowel movement and you are aware of it, a larger picture forms in your mind as to who your baby is and how she behaves. My friend Elizabeth points out that so many parents wish their newborns came with an instruction manual because they are so mysterious to them. Well, the more you learn about her elimination, eating, sleeping, and other preferences, the less mysterious your little baby will seem to you! Every bit of information will tell you more and more about who this little person is and how she likes to do things.

If you do find yourself feeling at all overwhelmed or frustrated, take a step back. Parents universally report that having a relaxed attitude to EC is paramount.

Parents Speak About Misses:

I like to think of misses as a "missed communication," like missing a friend's phone call. It seems like a friendlier way of looking at it than using the term "accident," which is commonly referred to in conventional toilet training. An "accident" sounds catastrophic; a friend's "missed call" can always be returned.

—ELIZABETH, MOM TO FELIX, 16, FRANKIE, 6, BEKAH, 5, LILLIAN, 2, AND JACK, 8 MONTHS

Because my baby was so much more comfortable when there were catches, I felt bad when there were misses, like I wasn't paying attention. But I also remind myself that as with anything in parenting, I'm doing the best I can. I've been in situations where I couldn't attend to her right away and would think, well, she has a diaper on; it's fine.

—KATE, MOM TO LUCIA, 6 MONTHS

With a three-month-old, you're constantly learning about him and getting it wrong some of the time. I don't feel EC is any more or less that way than anything else. When things are overwhelming, we just don't do it at that moment.

—ERIK, DAD TO XANDER, 3 MONTHS

Sometimes we have more misses than catches, so we just change the diaper and move on. I just lay off and forget about EC for a while, like until the next nap or the next day.

—EMILY, MOM TO OSCAR, 6 MONTHS

IF YOUR BABY ACTS FUSSY

Some newborns may act quite distressed by the act of going to the bathroom. It's a new and sometimes uncomfortable sensation for them. If faced with this situation, you have a couple of options. You can begin putting baby in the newborn in-arms hold right away and hold him over a bowl, toilet, or sink (yes, a sink; you can easily disinfect it afterward, and the height of a sink makes it an ideal place to potty a newborn!), but if your baby is still so young that he is disturbed by the change of position or the feeling of air on his body, you can simply cradle him in your arms over a loose diaper (or even not so loose, though loose makes it easier for you to confirm he's going) and cue him. Keep in mind, *where he goes does not matter.* What is important is that you are helping him form associations between his elimination and your cueing, your sound, and your reassuring, gentle presence. There is time enough in the future for him to start transferring that association to a specific position or place, such as a potty. Right now, the most important thing is to just let him know that you are there, that you are as aware as he is that he's going to the bathroom, and that you are helping him with his desire not to soil himself.

Some babies will cry right when they are about to go to the bathroom (or even during). This can be very confusing for you as a parent. Sometimes you may wonder if the baby is actually crying precisely because you are trying to potty her! In reality, many babies do cry when they are going to the bathroom, and we are just not aware of it if they are being diapered full-time. I've spoken to many parents, in fact, who say that their baby's "colic" symptoms disappeared once they started pottying them, because they were actually crying about the need to go to the bathroom.

The sensation of having to go to the bathroom and the feeling of releasing it can be frightening to a small baby, especially if she has been going in a diaper and is still fighting against that natural instinct not to soil herself. She also may not feel completely secure in the position in which you are holding her. This is a phenomenon that generally dissipates with time. You can always experiment with other positions, or cue your baby to go in a diaper, before trying that position again when baby is a bit older. Be reassuring and loving the entire time and hold her close in your arms.

If the crying persists or if your baby is quite obviously distressed, this may be a sign that she is experiencing some physical discomfort related to the act of elimination itself. It is important to remain watchfully observant and ask your doctor if you have any concerns. I know a doctor who actually figured out through EC that her baby had a urinary tract infection before the baby even presented with a fever. Other possible explanations for the crying are that your baby dislikes the feel of air on her naked body (keep the room warm and most of her body bundled up as best you can, whether you are changing her diaper or practicing EC) or that she has a red or raw bottom because of diaper rash. If the latter reason is the case, keep in mind that EC is the very best way to prevent diaper rash! The feeling of pee on those raw, irritated skin surfaces can be painful until she heals. At least you can minimize the amount of time she spends sitting in a dirty diaper if you EC.

EC is also beneficial because it allows you to pinpoint exactly what triggers your baby's crying. If your newborn is in a diaper and you are unaware she is eliminating, you might not be certain what is causing those wails. Many parents also have the opportunity to determine if their children are reacting to certain foods by observing the way their children act when going to the bathroom, how often they go to the bathroom, or even the appearance of their bowel movements. From a health perspective, therefore, EC provides parents with important information about their babies.

Parents Speak About How EC Made Their Newborns Happier:

> My baby was eleven weeks old when I heard about EC. He had experienced eight weeks of severe diaper rash and was in so much pain. Everyone kept telling me to leave his diaper off to air him out. As soon as I learned about EC and started doing it, he had no more diaper rash at all. Those eight weeks before EC were the most miserable weeks of his life.
>
> —JENNA, MOM TO DAVID, 10 MONTHS

> Since my baby was born, she really struggled with bowel movements. We had thought she was constipated, but really she just has a hard time going when she has a bowel movement. She would cry two or three times a day. We tried all sorts of things—I rubbed her stomach, pushed her little legs up on her stomach, everything. Nothing solved it but EC'ing her in the in-arms position.
>
> —AMYLYNNE, MOM TO MEREDITH, 4 MONTHS

> Lucia was miserable every time she would wet her diapers. It got to the point that when she cried, the first thing I would do was check to see if she needed to be changed. When we started EC'ing at six weeks old, that all changed almost immediately. She became a much happier baby overall and cried a lot less.
>
> —KATE, MOM TO LUCIA, 6 MONTHS

> Ben cried at random intervals all day long, and grunted all the time too, as if constipated. The first time I tried EC at two months, we caught a poop, and my son turned his head toward

me and gave me a huge smile. I was hooked and went to a DiaperFreeBaby meeting. I was told that EC isn't an alternative to potty training; it's an alternative way of thinking about elimination.

—SARABETH, MOM TO BEN, 8 MONTHS

Both of my children popped on and off the breast during nursing sessions. With the first, I thought it was a milk-supply problem, so I even tried pumping and giving her bottles. With my second, when she did the exact same thing, it finally occurred to me to take her to the bathroom—and then she was satisfied. Lots of babies pop on and off the breast at this age, and their moms are told it's a nursing issue. In my experience, it was an EC signal.

—KEILA, MOM TO HELEN, 27 MONTHS,
AND JANE, 8 MONTHS

Our baby had a UTI, which the doctor told us was most likely from a poopy diaper. No matter how diligently we cleaned her and how immediately we changed her, this could still happen. To add insult to injury, the antibiotics that she needed completely changed her rhythms; she was pooping constantly and developed a horrible red, raw diaper rash from all the pooping and wiping and the diapers.

When we finally started EC, she looked at me as if she were saying, "What took you so long?" and promptly pooped in the toilet. Suddenly there was no big clean up, no anguishing over "cracks and crevices"—just a little toilet paper and a flush.

—THEMBI, MOM TO NINA, 10 MONTHS

During the first few months of her life, Neshama would struggle during nursing at times, popping on and off the breast and appearing terribly uncomfortable. Within a couple of days after beginning EC, I realized that pulling off the breast was one of her most reliable cues for needing to pee, poop, or pass gas. Once we made that discovery, we never had that problem again.

—LAMELLE, MOM TO NESHAMA, 12 MONTHS

CLEANING UP AFTER BABY

While commercial wipes are useful, it's not that necessary to use them on your baby's tender skin, especially if you're practicing EC and your baby's skin is not getting that dirty anyway. If you do use wipes, a few pats will probably suffice. Many parents quickly rinse their babies off in a sink or a bathtub. I know one parent who keeps a small watering can near the toilet so she can just rinse her baby off that way with comfortable, room-temperature water. Others keep a little pile of flannel cloths or washcloths nearby for quick little wipe-ups or to pat baby's bottom dry.

LET'S REVIEW STARTING OUT:
THE BASICS

- Set aside some times to keep baby loosely diapered or diaper-free so you can check easily and observe her signs

- Cue her as soon as you notice she's going. Hold her in position and go *"pssst"* or make any other cue sounds that you want her to associate with peeing and pooping. She doesn't necessarily need to be diaperless for this when you're first starting out

- Place a tiny bowl, loose diaper, or Potty Bowl in your lap, or hold baby over a toilet or sink. Have a variety of positions in your repertoire until you settle on which positions she prefers (and keep in mind that her preferred positions may change over time)

• If you notice that she's already gone to the bathroom, change her as soon as possible so she doesn't become too conditioned to the feeling of sitting in a wet or dirty diaper

TUNING IN TO BABY'S PATTERNS AND SIGNALS

Although people tend to think that newborns just go to the bathroom at random throughout the day (and it certainly can be somewhat erratic at the beginning), newborns actually begin to settle into discernible patterns fairly soon. As I will mention throughout the book, it is fairly common for babies to go more often in the morning than in the afternoon, right after awakening from a nap, and several minutes after (or during) a feed. They may also continue to pee soon after you remove their diaper. By the same token, babies are less likely to spontaneously go to the bathroom if they are asleep, in arms, or in any upright position where they are not comfortable going to the bathroom (such as in a car seat). This doesn't mean that they *won't* go to the bathroom, but that they may fuss in an obvious way before doing so.

In any case, when thinking about times to offer your baby the potty, consider these typical times because you will likely have a higher chance of cueing or catching a pee or poop. (Remember though that all babies are different and that yours may have her own unique patterns.) Each time you perform a successful cue or catch, you build up a loose awareness of your baby's patterns, your baby learns what you are helping her with, and the two of you feel more in sync.

If you're just starting out, you may decide to use one of these typical times to give your baby a little diaper-free (or loose diaper) time so that you can concentrate on observing what her signals and cues might be right before she goes to the bathroom. If she tends to awaken in a good mood, you can take her out of her diaper, put a loose diaper under her or hold her over a bowl while she's cradled in your arms, and see what her behavior is like. She may shiver, spit up, look intent, or start squirming and grunting. Your baby is going to have her own individual way of expressing the impending need to go to the bathroom. Once you recognize the signs your baby makes, you can start to look out for these signs at other times as well.

At first, EC does require the willingness to spend some time just observing. It's a nice chance to slow down during those hectic newborn days. I just spent some time with a three-month-old EC'ed baby. His father held him in-arms over the toilet and the baby just quietly hung out there, gazing around, enjoying all of us watching. Suddenly he stopped looking at us, started to squirm, moved his arms a bit, fussed for a few seconds, and then—he peed!

Some parents may feel that no matter how much they observe their baby, they aren't really seeing any obvious signals or cues. Or they may see signs but not every time, not enough to feel that they can rely on them. If so, you can rely more on timing—simply noticing when your baby tends to go—and then remain open to the possibility that as your baby grows older, it will become easier to read her bodily cues.

Keep your intuition well honed; many parents find that a combination of timing and intuition (just a feeling that your baby probably needs to go to the bathroom) works well for them without explicitly looking for signals from the baby herself.

Newborns grow so quickly! Once your baby is starting to enjoy more time on her tummy or on the floor playing with toys, you may find that you need to figure out some new ways to tell if she has to go to the bathroom. When your baby is no longer in your arms as much or becomes distracted by toys, you may have a period of increased misses until you are both used to a new rhythm. But remember to think of misses as a normal part of life with an EC'ing baby; keep a relaxed attitude about them.

Martha was two weeks old when we started. It went very well—she just seemed to know what to do. I felt as though this was fulfilling her expectations, and it was actually I, not she, who was learning. (Our older two children were conventionally potty trained.) I was still at the stage of constantly staring at her and checking her, getting to know her in that all-absorbed way you do with your newborn. It's a good time to learn about her elimination needs—it just felt like another thing that you naturally learn about your baby, along with learning when to feed, when to comfort, when to help her sleep, etc.

—PAULA, MOM TO ELLIE, 4, JOE, 3,
AND MARTHA, 2 MONTHS

EC'ing my newborn (the second child I've EC'ed from birth) is going great. She sleeps all the time, so it's easy to potty her when she wakes up, and I have a Potty Bowl nearby so I don't have to go all the way to the bathroom to potty her. EC is going so well that we've been changing diapers only because she's been in them for a whole day rather than because they are wet! Even her grandma has peed her with success, and she and I are both amazed at how the baby fusses and fusses until she starts to pee. We can feel her relax when she lets it all go. So sweet for someone so tiny.

—KYLENE, MOM TO CAMERON, 5, EDDY, 2,
AND MARGARET, 4 DAYS OLD

On the day that Jason was born, catching that first pee was a high. Then to catch a meconium bowel movement and not have to clean up a tarry mess off of delicate skin hooked me! I felt in sync right away, as compared to my first child, who was conventionally potty trained.

—KATHERINE, MOM TO JEFFERSON, 4,
AND JASON, 14 MONTHS

PARENTS' FAVORITE EC'ING POSITIONS FOR NEWBORNS

- Sitting facing the toilet with baby cradled in arms

- Over a Potty Bowl (or other container or bowl)

- In a loose diaper while baby is cradled in arms

- Over the sink, shower, or bath tub drain (many babies like over the sink because they can see the mirror)

- Squatting outdoors (this can be done very discreetly, since baby is covered by your body)

- In a potty (for bigger babies)

TROUBLESHOOTING Q AND A

Q. I'm having a really hard time holding my newborn in position to pee or poop. She is so tiny and it feels very awkward.

A. I know—at first, EC (and everything else!) can feel awkward with a newborn. How do you position baby, wipe after a poop, clean up a loose diaper or bowl that's been pooped in while holding her, and hold her correctly? If you're finding it hard to get the hang of holding her in the EC positions, start out by letting her lie diaper-free on a loose cloth or disposable diaper, then cue when you see her going. You can gradually experiment with new positions as she gets bigger and you gain more confidence. If you're spending a lot of time holding her, you can even hold her on top of a few cloth diapers and pull the top layer off if she soils it. If you don't want your baby totally diaper-free, place her in a diaper and wrap her in a blanket (or use BabyLegs or socks to keep her legs warm). This will help avoid the hassle of taking all her clothes off to figure out whether she's going to the bathroom. Having a partner nearby to help with positioning or to take away a bowl to clean is also helpful while you are first getting the hang of EC. With practice and experience, things will seem more effortless.

Q. My newborn, a boy, sprays everywhere when I try to pee him in a bowl or potty. It feels awkward to pee him and try to aim his penis at the same time. Any tips?

A. Not all parents of boys experience this (individual anatomy seems to come into play), but those who do say that holding your baby while aiming his penis downward with your index finger as he's peeing will do the trick. If you are holding your baby under his thighs in the newborn EC position, your index finger ought to be able to reach over from under his thighs and help aim things in the right direction. As he gets older and sits on a potty or toilet, you may still help aim his penis until he is able to do it on his own. In general, these pee-aiming issues will resolve when he's no longer such a small baby.

Q. My child always poops while nursing. How can I EC her at these times?

A. It's very common for newborns, whether they're being EC'ed or not, to poop in the middle of a nursing session. Some babies will signal the impending elimination need by popping on and off the breast and appearing fussy or uncomfortable. They are more comfortable being held to poop, and then returning to the nursing session. Keep in mind that sometimes a poop can last a long time! With observation, you will begin to learn when your baby is fully done. There are also many babies who are most comfortable if you continue to nurse them while holding them. Since the newborn positions call for babies to be cradled in your arms, this is not difficult and a little practice or adjustment is all it takes. Be assured, they won't always poop while nursing.

SIGNS THAT YOUR BABY HAS TO GO TO THE BATHROOM

- Spitting up

- Passing gas

- Squirming

- Straining

- Any change in behavior (sudden fussiness, suddenly quiet after babbling, just seeming unsettled)

- Timing (after naps, before and after going out)

- Shivering

- Kicking legs

- Looking at you

- Popping off the breast while nursing

TYPICAL TIMES FOR NEWBORNS TO GO TO THE BATHROOM

- Upon awakening

- After coming out of a sling or car seat

- Before, after, or during a feed

- When diaper comes off for a diaper change

Parents Speak About Starting to EC a Newborn:

My son was just under three months old when we started. I was doing it part-time, and I tried to give him a few hours of diaper-free time every day. I think that because we started so slowly, it didn't feel overwhelming. I just looked at our diaper-free time as a way to get in touch, and mostly just took note of when he peed, if he had any signals, etc. I also only did it when we were at home, at first, so we didn't have to deal with what other people thought.

—STACY, MOM TO ORLANDO, 30 MONTHS

I found it much easier in the first few weeks to use no diapers, because diapers don't really fit such small new babies, and you have to change them so frequently. We kept Jasmine on top of a large prefold diaper with a wool pad underneath it. It was so easy to just slide the flat diaper out from under her and slide in the new one. We learned her patterns and signals more easily and were catching most of her poops and pees. We found it to be cleaner and a lot more efficient to invest the time and energy up front in taking her to the potty, rather than having to clean up soiled diapers and her bottom.

—BRIDGET, MOM TO CARLY, 5, AND JASMINE, 3

I learned a lot of things about my son through EC. For those first months, it was all such a guessing game: was he tired? Hungry? Cold? Hot? It was anyone's best guess, and even after I'd do something for him, I was never quite sure whether he really had been hungry or thirsty or whatever. But with this potty thing, it was a definite yes or no proposition. What a relief! Now we had a developing language, and our first word was *"pssss."*

—SARABETH, MOM TO BEN, 8 MONTHS

I conventionally toilet trained my first two children. So far, EC with my third child is far easier and feels much more natural. Now that I've started, it feels very similar to breastfeeding on cue, in that I do it without really consciously thinking about it.

Sometimes, especially when I'm busily interacting with the other two at the same time, I've undressed baby, held her on the bowl for a pee, and dressed her without really realizing I was doing it. Similar to looking down during a conversation and noticing you're already feeding the baby!

—PAULA, MOM TO MARTHA, 2 MONTHS

EXPANDING EC AS YOU GET IN SYNC

Up to now, if you're new to EC and still getting to know your newborn, chances are that you have been practicing it either as an occasional or a part-time EC'er. However, as you start to connect with your baby, you may be expanding the times when you practice EC, and may feel like moving on to full-time EC will work for you. Families that started out catching only bowel movements may decide to try catching some pees as well. Others who have practiced EC throughout the day here or there may decide that they will start doing it on the go or at nighttime. If you are using disposables but are noticing that you are catching a high percentage of your baby's output, this may also be a chance for you to switch to cloth training pants or something else at least part of the time.

When we started EC with my first daughter, we were using disposables. But I was constantly wondering if I was putting on a wet diaper or throwing away a perfectly clean diaper. So then I started buying cloth diapers and using those.

—KEILA, MOM TO HELEN, 27 MONTHS,
AND JANE, 8 MONTHS

EC'ING YOUR NEWBORN AT NIGHT AND ON THE GO

At Night

New parents experience interrupted sleep with newborns—this is a part of life. If you are going to be up doing diaper changes or nursing anyway, you might consider cueing your baby at nighttime as well. This is a personal choice. Some parents feel that they don't want to EC at nighttime and are just happy to be moving out of frequent diaper changes as the baby gets older. They may decide that nighttime EC will make more sense for them as their baby gets older, especially if their baby is not visibly distressed by elimination in a diaper at night, or they may never do it. Other parents might practice EC one, two, or more times a night with a baby who settles back into sleep happily after being EC'ed. They might keep baby in a diaper but cue the baby—either in a diaper or in a container nearby—followed by a diaper change, so that the baby can comfortably go back to sleep again. A dim nightlight for this purpose is helpful, so that no bright lights need to be turned on that would be stimulating for the baby (or for you!). Others might decide to keep their baby minimally diapered, if at all, at nighttime, and keep the baby on top of a fleece pad to soak up any misses that might occur.

On the Go

EC'ing on the go may feel daunting, but with newborns, just about everything has a learning curve. That is part of what makes this stage so overwhelming and yet so exciting. Figure out which positions your baby prefers and bring along a small container, keeping a few extra containers and diapers in the car or in your diaper bag. The more adept you become at EC, the fewer actual diapers you will probably be stocking in your diaper bag!

Babies can be sensitive to changes in their environment, but this is true for all aspects of their lives, such as eating and sleeping, not just elimination. This is particularly true if going on extended overnight trips. Remain aware of how your baby is reacting to his new environment and accommodate him.

Some people find that travel, especially, is a good time to practice EC because they have more time and energy to focus on the baby. It can actually jump-start some people who only practice EC occasionally to try it more often. Others find that it throws them off and that it takes some time to get back in sync with the baby's rhythms. If this happens, be assured that it's not at all uncommon; just do what you need to do to make your lives run smoothly. Keep your baby in diapers for now, and tell yourself that you and your baby will have many other opportunities again in the near future.

> The first couple of days we tried EC, I didn't feel like we were getting anywhere, although I did catch one or two pees. Then, my husband, the baby, and I went away for a week. Where we stayed there was a little plastic potty that Oscar could sit on, and when we offered it to him, he used it a lot. We started with timing-based offers. After we started to get some signals, we took off his dry diapers and were able to catch some pees. It went really well.
>
> —EMILY, MOM TO OSCAR, 6 MONTHS

You've laid down a lot of foundations through EC'ing your newborn. You've learned to trust your instincts, to read your baby's cues, and to figure out his patterns. Your baby's also learned to trust that you are there to help respond to his needs. He's been able to maintain the bodily awareness he was born with and he can make associations between your cues and his elimination. Now let's move on to the next chapter in your journey, as you and your baby continue to enjoy and deepen the EC'ing relationship you've cultivated.

5

EC'ing During Middle Infancy: Smooth Sailing

Your baby is no longer a newborn, and now you're enjoying a new, precious stage as you parent your lovable, happy, responsive, and curious little baby. Many EC'ing families begin shortly before or just around this stage. For some of them, it's taken this long to get settled as a newly expanded family after the birth. Others may not have discovered EC until now. In any case, it's a great time to get started. Middle infancy—about three to eight months, or the period from when your child has more neck control to when he becomes mobile—really is an ideal time to practice elimination communication.

Whether you're just starting out or have been following EC since your baby was born, there are characteristics about middle infancy that make EC go particularly smoothly during this period. Your baby is more aware of the world around her and is more responsive to you, so it's easy for the two of you to get in tune with one another. She's stronger and may even be able to sit up now, making positioning easier, but she's not yet mobile, so she's probably often nearby and not as distractible as she will be later on. Babies often fall into more predictable routines at this point as well, and their cues may become more obvious.

Remember the three tracks I mentioned in the first chapter: full-time EC, part-time EC, and occasional EC. These are just general guidelines to help you figure out which sections of this book are most helpful to you. They are not categories meant to pigeonhole you in any way. Naturally, I expect that you will probably shift back and forth between categories throughout the EC journey, even from day to day or week to week. The most important part of each and every track is that your goal be to simply tune in to your baby and listen to what she is telling you. It is not about having a baby who goes X number of times a day on a potty, or having a perfect track record, or getting your baby out of diapers before anyone else. Remember, elimination communication is first and foremost about communication!

For those of you who began practicing EC with your newborns, congratulations on making it to the next stage. You probably still have misses or don't necessarily catch every pee, but you may be so aware of your baby's patterns and signals that you've developed an intuitive sense for when your baby is likely to need to go to the bathroom, and it's feeling more and more like a way of life for you. I think you'll find this chapter useful in learning about the unique advantages and challenges of practicing EC in middle infancy.

STARTING OUT
Strategies and Cues

If you're just starting out, you have a couple of options about how best to begin. An easy and helpful way to start is to take your baby's diaper off for an hour or two. Spend a little time observing your baby, seeing if she signals, and cueing her (*"psss!"*) if she does go, so that she develops an association between cueing and going. Remember how

I described how to cue, in chapter 4? If you catch your baby starting to pee or poop, make a sound or say a word that you've already chosen. (*"Psss!"* is a common one, or you can say *"pee pee"* or *"tsss"* or whatever comes naturally to you. If your baby is having a bowel movement, a common cue is to make a modified grunting noise.) Keep repeating your cue sounds while your baby is going to the bathroom.

A lot of parents may already have developed some awareness of their baby's patterns even without any prior knowledge of EC. You might have noticed your baby tends to poop a couple of times in a row in the morning, for instance. Use this knowledge to determine when might be an optimal time of day to have your baby go diaper-free.

To make diaper-free time comfortable, you can create a cozy little place for her to lie down using a fleece waterproof pad with a few of her favorite toys scattered around. Or, if she's a cuddlebug who loves spending time in your arms, you can place a diaper between her legs without fastening it. (If you're using a disposable diaper and it's hard to tell if she's gone, you could consider putting a cloth liner, a washcloth, or a little piece of tissue in there to make it easier.) Remember to cue and talk to her whenever you notice she is going to the bathroom. All that acknowledgment helps her to maintain the bodily awareness she was born with, and you'll both benefit from this later in the process.

Babies are so amazing! They catch on to what you're doing very quickly. When you make your cueing sound around the time that your baby probably needs to go anyway, your baby will connect the sound with the sensation of going to the bathroom. In the meantime, you'll have had a chance to see what kind of behavior your baby may exhibit right before or during a pee or poop. She might be grimacing, fussing, squirming, or, conversely, going totally still. She might be vocalizing, grunting, or straining. Try taking her to the bathroom the next time you notice such signs, especially if you know she hasn't gone in a little while, and make your cueing sound. See what happens. More likely than not, she will eliminate! And any time you respond to her in this way, she will learn to trust that you are there for her and are helping her with her needs.

Introducing the Potty or Toilet

Another way to get started is to put your baby right on a potty soon after drinking, eating, or waking to see what happens; again, cue if you notice the baby going. You can introduce a potty at this age with great success. Since your baby is sitting up (or nearly so), she'll definitely be comfortable on one, although she will still need your support to help her stay on at the beginning. Of course, little babies aren't going to be all that comfortable on a large potty made for toddlers, and they don't need all the little gimmicks (like a lid or a potty

that plays music when it gets wet, for instance) that manufacturers often include to make toilet training appeal to an older child. There are lots of potties on the market; choose your potty carefully. The Baby Bjorn Little Potty was seemingly made especially for infants; it allows them to sit in a squat with their feet on the floor and won't tip

Four-month-old Hilary on the potty

Signs That Your Baby Has to Use the Potty

- Sudden fussiness or squirming

- Wiggling, kicking

- Arching the back when being held

- A blank expression or frown on the face

- A certain vocalization (that babies may be doing to try to imitate your own cue sound); this is going to be unique to each baby

- Moving toward a potty, playing with a clean potty, staring at a potty or at the bathroom door

- Signing ASL for "potty"

- Timing (right after a meal, before or after outings, after naps)

- Intuition (a sudden feeling your baby probably has to go; this is usually also based on a loose, unconscious awareness of baby's timing and when he last went)

- Shivering

- Blowing raspberries

- Passing gas

- For boys, a slightly swollen penis

- "Warning" pees—a slight discharge of urine shortly before a real pee

- "Phantom pees"—if baby is worn on you, a feeling of warmth even if baby hasn't gone yet—especially if baby is diaper-free

over. (Not coincidentally, this position is one that many toddlers instinctively use to poop in, even when wearing a diaper!) The transparent Babywunder Deluxe Clear Potty is great too because it allows you to tell if your baby has gone or not without disturbing her position. And stock up on potties if you can—EC is so much easier if your equipment is within reach. Just as nursing moms are often advised to create "nursing stations" in their homes, you can also create little "potty stations." By keeping a potty close by in most of the rooms you spend time in (the nursery, your bedroom, the playroom, and, of course, the bathroom!), you will feel more motivated to help your child eliminate outside of a diaper.

It's not too soon to use an actual toilet, either. The newborn in-arms position over a toilet, as discussed in chapter 4, is still a good position for your older baby to go in. (I still hold my three-year-old this way if I don't want him to come into contact with a dirty public toilet. It's really convenient that he has always been comfortable in this position.) This position is, of course, adaptable; some parents find it works best to sit straddling the toilet with baby right in front of them. But bigger babies are actually now able to go onto the toilet with a seat insert, although you need to stay nearby and support their bodies.

Summary of Positions

- Newborn in-arms hold over a toilet, sink, or bowl

- Potty sitting position

- Parent straddling the toilet and holding baby

- Baby on toilet alone (with seat insert, and holding parent's hand)

Parents can sit on the toilet with their baby or toddler, either facing the toilet or facing out.

Neshama, ten months, bonding with Mommy while on the toilet

The newborn in-arms position

Starting Slow

If you're the type that likes to plunge right in, more power to you! However, I like to recommend starting out slowly, with low expectations, especially if you're new to this. Small successes are so encouraging. Starting out small might mean that you begin by aiming for one opportunity a day (notice that I say opportunity, not necessarily a catch)—say, right before bath time, or after a nap. Make it your aim to let your baby enjoy a bit of time on the potty with a toy. Or you could take her diaper off for a little bit and just see where that takes you. Many EC'ers also recommend simply putting your baby over the potty whenever you happen to be changing her diaper. This really takes no extra effort if her diaper is already off and you have a potty right by the changing table. Remember: if you catch her peeing, even if not into an actual potty, don't forget to make your cue sound! And stay positive and affirming. This is a matter-of-fact bodily function that comes naturally to your baby. You want her to associate toilet time with loving, bonding time with you.

How long should you keep your baby on the potty? You will quickly develop a sense for this. Most experienced EC'ers find that they know within a few seconds whether the baby will have to go. If your baby is fine in the position but not going to the bathroom, this may mean she needs a bit of time to relax her muscles and release her pee. Cue her (*"psss!"*) while you are waiting, as the association she's already formed will help her to go. If your baby looks away, does not look intent, or even squirms out of your arms, this is very likely a sign that she is not interested and doesn't need to use the toilet at that time. However, there may also be a period of time before baby gets accustomed to the new potty or in-arms position, especially if she is an older baby, when she may act somewhat squirmy or resistant, even if she does have to go. Remember to introduce her slowly and gently, backing off if she seems uncomfortable.

If your baby is very resistant to the idea of sitting on the potty or in the in-arms position over the toilet, consider giving her some diaper-free time over a fleece pad on the floor, during which you can cue her if she happens to go. This way she will be able to associate the cueing sound with going to the bathroom, which is a crucial first step to regaining the bodily awareness she was born with.

Making the Most of Potty Time

While your baby is on the potty or toilet, you can play with her, sing to her, and talk to her. She'll associate potty time with the wonderful opportunity to be face-to-face with you and share some special moments. One friend of mine has a sweet little song she sings when the baby's on the toilet. (She remembers her own mother singing to her when she herself was being toilet trained!) If you're interested in other ways to communicate with your baby, you could start practicing some baby sign language. At the very least, teach her the American Sign Language (ASL) sign for toilet (see Resources for a website with an online demonstration of the sign). This will come in handy later on, as quite a few older babies and toddlers signal that they have to go to the bathroom by making this sign well before they are verbal. How well I remember the amazing sight of my little toddler—barely even walking yet—suddenly signing "toilet" to me from across the room!

Cleaning Up the Potty

Every parent has his or her own cleaning method, but many parents simply dump the contents of the potty into the toilet, quickly wipe the potty with toilet paper if necessary after a bowel movement, and then spray with a cleaner or disinfectant and wipe dry. I also rinsed the potty with hot running water before spraying in a little cleaner and letting it air-dry.

Parents Speak About Beginning EC in Middle Infancy:

We were all in cloth diapers when we were young, and after every meal, our diapers would be taken off. My grandmother (who helped take care of us) would make the cueing sound. It just seemed like a pretty painless way to toilet train. With Anna, I noticed that when she started solids she went more regularly, and she'd go in a sitting position, as if she were sitting in a high chair and had just finished a meal. So if it looked like she needed to go, I'd put her on the potty.

—ANGELINE, MOM TO ANNA, 10 MONTHS

Veda's babysitter is a sixty-year-old woman from India who said that you just hold babies over a bowl to get them used to going outside a diaper. We started when our baby could hold her head up. We thought we'd start once a day. In the afternoon we would give her juice at around four o'clock and wait a little while with the bowl. We made it fun reading time, and she always produced the goods.

—ASMIRA, MOM TO VEDA, 16 MONTHS

Gabriella brought us to EC by her refusal to soil a diaper. Eight days, no poop. I was online doing various searches and saw something about elimination communication/infant potty training. When Gabriella would only poop over a diaper but never *in* a diaper, I had one of those "aha" moments wondering why I was holding her over a diaper when I could just as easily be holding her over a toilet. The same positions that are encouraged with EC are the positions I was instinctively using to help her to go.

—SUZANNE, MOM TO GABRIELLA, 16 MONTHS

I already knew when Haakon was going poop, and it seemed strange and counterintuitive to just watch him poop all over himself and wait for him to finish in order to clean him up. Within a couple days of when we started, he knew what to do when I cued him. It was amazing. It was like he had been expecting this all along and seemed to understand the cue sound as if it were instinctive to him.

—DARA, MOM TO HAAKON, 8 MONTHS

We actually started EC when Zoe was born but took a break after a while because we felt overwhelmed. When she started to eat solids, though, I recommitted to EC because it was such a relief not to have those poops go in a diaper. And she hated having her diaper changed, so it was good for both of us.

—HAYA, MOM TO ZOE, 12 MONTHS

Baby's Signals

The most exciting part of EC at this stage may be that your baby is probably signaling more on her own when she has to go to the bathroom.

At 8 months, my daughter would usually tell me when she had to pee by rubbing her nose.

—LAMELLE, MOM TO NESHAMA, 12 MONTHS

My baby was actually signaling me during the day, letting me know she had to go by crawling into the potty, crawling into the bathroom and picking up the potty, or telling me if she'd made a puddle on the floor.

—LARA, MOM TO RUBY, 12 MONTHS

Every time he goes I make a sound while he's sitting on the potty. Lately, while he's going to the bathroom, he imitates the sound. I'm hoping that he will eventually make that sound before he has to go.

—SABA, MOM TO KENAN, 7 MONTHS

It was amazing, something I will always remember, communicating with such a tiny newborn. He signed ASL for potty at just a few months old! It gave me a lot of confidence in our bond: that he would let me know what he needed and that I could understand him and meet his needs.

—DIANA, MOM TO DORIAN, 7 MONTHS

At one point, Haakon was lying on my lap nursing. Suddenly, he looked me straight in the eye and patted his diaper area. I thought, Oh, I'm probably making this up, but it really looks like he's telling me he has to pee! So I brought him to the bathroom, and sure enough, he went straightaway and continued to do this a few more times that day. He will also look toward the bathroom or reach out for the potty.

—DARA, MOM TO HAAKON, 8 MONTHS

Do keep in mind that not all babies signal or signal in ways that we can pick up. Don't feel discouraged if your baby falls into this category. His signals may be subtle, or he may not be signaling in a way that you can discern; this is something that may happen later on for him. All babies are unique. Just remember that by being aware of his patterns and giving him opportunities to go to the bathroom, you're keeping up your side of the communication.

Feeling Discouraged?

If you feel like you are constantly trying to catch a pee but are getting to your baby just *after* she has gone to the bathroom in her diaper; if you notice that she is holding her bladder while on the potty (because she is so used to eliminating only in a diaper); or if you just have no idea what signals she might be giving off, then it might help to invest a little time in letting her go completely diaperless and observing her. At some point, she'll go to the bathroom and you can make your cue sound (*"psss!"*). Soon you'll both catch on.

Parents Speak About Part-Time EC:

I am following EC part-time, and it's going well. I catch most of Soren's poops in a regular toilet—it's so much easier. I catch some pees too, but I just can't be on top of all of them and feel stress-free about it. I was occasionally feeling bad that Soren is not diaper-free yet, but then I realized it's all a growing communication. We've got our poop communication down, and the other will come when we are both ready for that commitment. At least we have a language together.

—VANESSA, MOM TO MARET, 2,
AND SOREN, 7 MONTHS

LET'S GO OVER THE TRACKS AGAIN

Track 1, Full-Time EC   By practicing EC day in and day out, you have gotten to know your baby's patterns pretty well by now, and your baby trusts that you're going to be helping her go to the bathroom in a potty or toilet much of the time. You're catching a lot of pees and bowel movements, and things are going smoothly. Many people switch to training pants or cloth diapers without a cover during this stage. They still go outside with a change of clothes and training pants, or maybe an extra diaper, but catches are pretty reliable, especially at home. If they're going through a stage where they're having more misses because of developmental growth spurts or illness, for example, they can use the "three-miss rule"—after three misses, baby goes back into a diaper for the rest of the day (or whatever time period suits them).

Track 2, Part-Time EC   You're probably giving your baby opportunities ("pottytunities") a couple times a day. Your baby may be in diapers full-time (although if he's going in the potty at times, you're going to need fewer diapers—what a nice bonus!). This is the time when, if you have an hour at home with a little time to just hang out with your baby, you could consider letting her go diaper-free for a bit, or you could put her in a training pant or a cloth diaper without a cover. Using one or two cloth diapers a day is not going to add much to your laundry and it's a great way for your baby to remain aware of her elimination.

Track 3, Occasional EC   Even once a day or once in a while is a great opportunity for your baby to get used to the potty and the concept of eliminating in it. Babies tend to most obviously signal when they're about to poop, so most parents on this track try catching poops first. The big advantage: you don't have to clean smeared poop off your baby! As my friend Rachel says, you actually come less into contact with poop when you're EC'ing because it goes right into the toilet or potty; you're not wiping gobs of it off your baby with a thin little wipe.

SPECIFIC ISSUES AND COMMON CONCERNS
EC on the Go

No matter how smoothly EC may be going in the comfort of your own home, it's a rare parent who isn't daunted at first by the prospect of EC'ing on the go. Dirty public toilets, friends who don't have a potty in their homes, public transportation, or being stuck in traffic—all this may be enough to make a parent just want to give up! It is, of course; an option to reserve EC for the times when you're home. Lots of EC'ing parents do this. Your baby is still going to remain aware if you're not applying EC everywhere you go. But if you are willing to try EC while you're out and about, there are plenty of parents out there who can assure you that incorporating the process into an active life is perfectly manageable.

Some parents travel with their babies in training pants and just take along a change of clothes. They offer a pottytunity before and after outings. For instance, if they're going out to a friend's house, they might offer the potty right before leaving (and also scout out the bathroom situation once they've arrived at their destination). Practice makes it a lot easier. My friend Dara potties her baby absolutely everywhere she goes. She's been doing it so long that she doesn't have to think twice, and she's more than comfortable pottying her baby in stores, restaurants, outdoors, at friends' houses, and so on.

My babies were fairly regular, so I knew their patterns well. Daniel would have a bowel movement early in the morning, and I could count on that being it for the rest of the day. He'd also have a couple pees in the morning and then be dry for a few hours at a time in the afternoon (a typical pattern for many babies, by the way). So I could loosely plan around this schedule and know that if I were going to go out in the morning, I should put him in a backup diaper. If it was during the afternoon, I could be pretty sure that, with a pee before and after going out, underwear or a training pant would more than suffice.

If this all sounds complicated, I can assure you that it was much less overwhelming than it might sound on paper. With surprisingly little practice, you're going to develop an intuitive, unconscious sense of your baby's patterns. In the same way that, when planning an outing, you take into consideration when your child is going to be hungry or sleepy, you will easily start to maintain a loose awareness of his elimination patterns.

Observing your baby's patterns is, again, important here. It's actually very typical for babies to hold their pee when they are in certain positions, such as when held in a sling or baby carrier. These are not physiologically conducive states for eliminating, and even a non-EC'ed baby is usually uncomfortable going in one of these positions.

It's just as important to be aware of the times your baby *doesn't* go to the bathroom as it is to keep track of the times she does go. This means that if you are taking a walk and your baby is in a sling, you can be pretty sure that you'll have a peeing opportunity right after you take her out of the sling. She probably will not go while snuggled against your body (especially if you offered her an opportunity before you left). This may also be the case if she's in a car seat or a stroller. In general, the more your baby gets used to going to the bathroom outside of a diaper, the more likely she is to signal her desire to go to the bathroom outside of a diaper.

There are always exceptions, however, and your own particular baby may actually tend to go to the bathroom in these situations. This is why it's so important to observe and take note of your child's patterns and tendencies. Sometimes, if you know you'll be in the car for a while, offering your child a preemptive pottytunity can help you avoid a miss while she's in the car seat.

While you may or may not need to take a fully stocked diaper bag out with you anymore, there are still some things you should have in your bag that make it easier to EC your baby on the go.

POSSIBLE CONTENTS OF AN EC "DIAPER" BAG

- A cup or plastic bottle with a lid (especially if you have a little boy)

- A Tupperware container or Potty Bowl

- A small portable potty if your child prefers a potty rather than the in-arms position over a toilet or a container

- An actual diaper or two if you plan to cue baby to go in a loosely fastened diaper (or are practicing EC part-time)

- A pair of training pants, depending on how EC is going for you, along with a change of pants

And if you use a car, be sure to keep a little potty in the trunk!

If all this brings up images of you dragging EC gear or a little potty around for months on end, remember that it's really not for all that long. As your baby gets a bit older, her sphincter muscles will naturally strengthen if she's been EC'ed, and in many cases she'll be able to wait until you take her to a bathroom. (Many parents report this happening as early as mid-infancy.) If you were conventionally training an older toddler or preschooler, you'd likely need to take some gear with you for a period of time as well, on top of having lugged around a fully-stocked diaper bag for all those years of diaper wearing.

Parents Speak About EC on the Go:

For us, being diaper-free means being free from an exclusive reliance on diapers. For the most part, we still use diapers when we leave the house, but we will often spend several hours out and return to find the same (dry) diaper. In general, I've always tried to give Neshama a chance to pee at transitional moments, like when she comes out of the car seat or the sling.

—LAMELLE, MOM TO NESHAMA, 12 MONTHS

When we're going out, we use a backup diaper, even though she doesn't need it seventy percent of the time. We use cloth diapers; sometimes we'll go out with a cover and sometimes without one. I usually put one on if I know it's going to be a long day away from home.

—LARA, MOM TO RUBY, 12 MONTHS

We were traveling down to Florida. I knew my baby would have to go so I held him over the toilet in the airplane, and he went. You know what it's like changing a diaper in the plane, and I knew I didn't want to do that. I had just fed him; I knew he'd have to go.

—SABA, MOM TO KENAN, 7 MONTHS

We went on a weeklong trip when Dexter was five months and only took the toilet seat reducer with us. My husband and I would potty the baby when we were near a bathroom. To our amazement, we didn't even use the diapers we had brought along! By this point he would wait until we got to a public restroom or the hotel room and then poop as soon as we put him on the toilet. He even went on the airplane toilet. It saved a ton of time and money not to change diapers.

—RIKKI, MOM TO DEXTER, 11 MONTHS

Since Nina was an infant, she generally hasn't wanted to go in her pants. I've been fortunate in that Nina can and will hold it in public, let me know, and give me plenty of time to get her to a bathroom. I keep a Baby Bjorn Little Potty in the car and offer it before we go inside (the store, the mall, a friend's house— wherever) and before we leave for home. If we're just visiting someone, I bring it inside. If we're at the mall or out and about, I have a folding potty that fits neatly inside my diaper bag and has disposable liners that I can toss in the trash. For the most part, though, she just goes less often when we're out. I always bring a change of clothing but have never had to use it.

—THEMBI, MOM TO NINA, 12 MONTHS

To me, one challenge of EC in a big city has been doing it discreetly in public if there's no bathroom nearby. Here are some of my thoughts on EC'ing in public:

• Keep a container, jar, potty, or bottle with you

• "Cover up" with the baby's dress or pants (pushed down just far enough) or with a blanket or a sling

• If using diaper backup, you can just pull the diaper down a little and cue your baby to go into it when you find yourself in a situation where you know baby has to pee but it would be hard to potty

• Offer pottytunities before leaving and when a bathroom is available, and change wet diapers as quickly as possible in between these times. Thinking of immediate diaper changes as "almost as good" as catches helped me stay relaxed

—ERIN, MOM TO EVE, 4, AND GRACE, 6 MONTHS

"Pottytunities," or Good Opportunities to Offer Your Baby a Chance to Use the Bathroom

• After waking

• During or after nursing

• During or after meals

• Before leaving the house

• After returning home

• Right after taking baby out of a sling, stroller, or car seat

• When changing baby's diaper

• Before or after a bath

• Before bed

EC AT NIGHTTIME

Ah, nighttime. It's crucial for parents to be well rested to function during the daytime, and you may be wondering if EC is at all compatible with a good night's sleep. It's usually the case that babies of this young age are not likely to stay dry all night, although a certain hormone, ADH, or antidiuretic hormone, is released during sleep and can help keep older babies and children dry for longer periods at naps or nighttime (this is why many babies—and adults!—pee as soon as they get up). It's not unheard of for nighttime dryness to occur before a year for some babies. But the reality is that a baby in middle infancy is probably going to pee at night. Whether and how to assist babies with their bathroom needs in the middle of the night is a very understandable question for all people who are intrigued by EC.

First of all, how you approach nighttime EC depends in some part on where your baby is sleeping and what your basic philosophies about infant sleep are. Are you co-sleeping in the same bed? Is he in a crib in the same room or sleeping in a separate room? Does he tend to wake at night for a quick nurse, comfort, or in response to the urge to pee, or does he sleep for long stretches? Based on these factors, you will figure out whether it makes sense for you to EC at night.

EC'ing at Night

Many people find that their babies may actually be night waking precisely because their need to go to the bathroom makes them uncomfortable. If this is the case for your baby, using the EC skills you've honed during the daytime may, in the long run, make for a better night's sleep. Taking her to the potty in a darkened room and then quietly getting her back to sleep can take just a minute or two.

If you're EC'ing at night, remember that there are lots of similarities to EC'ing in the daytime. You don't have to try to catch every pee. You will probably develop some sense of your baby's patterns and timing. You may notice that your baby tends to pee while night nursing, for instance. And you may notice that the quicker you meet this nursing and elimination need, the quicker your baby drops off to sleep again. Moreover, many families who EC at night feel that nighttime EC goes more smoothly than daytime EC because there are fewer distractions.

You're probably wondering how EC'ers handle the logistics of nighttime. Most people put a waterproof pad under the sheet where their baby is sleeping. On top of this they may put a large fleece or woolen puddle pad. Many parents keep a little potty by the bed for quick pottying. To streamline things further, they might put a cloth or disposable diaper inside the potty to absorb the pee so that they don't have to go all the way to the bathroom to empty it. Some parents will leave their baby diaperless at night because they have developed such a reliable, mutual communication with their baby about her elimination needs. Others will put their baby in a diaper even if they will probably be catching most nighttime pees.

> At night, her signs were so obvious; she'd wake me to go. It just seemed to me that she'd be more comfortable sleeping without a diaper, so I took it off and let her go diaper-free. She always wakes me to go potty so she doesn't have to wet the bed. After doing this at night, I decided to start practicing EC during the daytime as well.
>
> —LARA, MOM TO RUBY, 12 MONTHS

We've done some form of nighttime EC since the beginning. I keep a potty, diapers, and wipes by the bed. If Neshama stirs during a nap or at night, she either wants to nurse, pee, or both. If she wakes up crying or tossing and turning, it's most likely because she has to pee. I simply take off her diaper, sit her on the potty, offer her the chance to nurse, whisper our tinkle song and give the cue, and she pees. This usually happens just once a night. Sometimes if we're less in sync, she'll wake up only after having gone in her diaper. I'll just quickly change her and we're back to sleep.

—LAMELLE, MOM TO NESHAMA, 12 MONTHS

Whereas daytime EC'ing can be all over the place, nights have always been stable. We started right away in that we kept his diaper dry by changing it at every feed during the newborn stage, giving him a pee break at changes. In the middle infancy stage I could tell he needed to go because he would squirm or kick.

—CHARNDRA, MOM TO MAVEN, 11 MONTHS

At night I practice EC whenever he wakes up. Nights are easiest for us because there are no distractions. He'll be sleeping soundly, then suddenly he'll start grunting and moving. When I take his diaper off, he'll smile; I'll walk him right over to the bathroom and give him the cue sound.

—KEVIN, DAD TO KAYDEN, 3 MONTHS

Not EC'ing at Night

Other parents may be intent on preserving the longer stretches of sleep that they have become accustomed to and look at nighttime EC as something that would possibly disrupt this cycle. They may even worry that EC'ing at night would be teaching the baby to wake up at night. In reality, most newborns will stir, even if just slightly, to pee. Eventually, a newborn may learn to sleep through that sensation and pee in his diaper. If you are reluctant to rekindle his awareness, let things continue on as they are in the daytime. Eventually, perhaps in the next stage or two (discussed later in this book), your child will either wake with a clearly expressed need to go to the bathroom and ask for your assistance, as happens with conventionally trained children, or your child will develop the physical capacity to stay dry at night.

We didn't do EC at night. He was diapered, and if he woke I would take him, but we didn't make night EC the priority. Sleep was the priority.

—KATHRYN, MOM TO FOUR CHILDREN, INCLUDING T. C., 3

He sleeps twelve hours straight; so there's no way I can take him to the potty then. After he wakes up with a wet diaper, I simply give him a few minutes and then take him to the potty.

—SABA, MOM TO KENAN, 7 MONTHS

We don't EC at night. I'm usually an all-or-nothing person, but in this case I know it is more important for me and my family that I get a good night's sleep. I am a much better mother when I am well rested.

—BETH, MOM TO ZEV, 9, ARAVA, 6, TEMIMA, 3,
AND EDEN, 4 MONTHS

Nighttime Setup

If you're EC'ing at nighttime, here are some strategies. Keep in mind safe-sleeping guidelines and be careful not to allow loose material near your young baby's face.

- Put a protective waterproof sheet under the bedsheet
- Use a large fleece or wool pad or a PULpad on top of the bedsheet
- Put a diaper or training pant on baby that is easy to change in the nighttime. Some parents have their babies lie diaperless on a loose prefold that they can just change if baby wets it. Again, if doing this, please keep safe-sleeping guidelines in mind.
- Keep a potty near the bed. Some people put a little diaper in the bottom to soak up any pee so you don't have to get up and empty until morning

Common Questions and Concerns Overheard at a DiaperFreeBaby Support Meeting

Q. "If my baby is going to the bathroom in different potties, toilets, sinks, even outdoors, how will he ever learn that the bathroom is the appropriate place to pee and poop?"

A. Your baby is still so very young. Likely he is still nursing or eating, maybe even sleeping, in different places. The important thing now is to help him retain his bodily awareness. It's not always possible for a child of this age to hold it until you can get him to an actual bathroom, and this would create unnecessary work for you too, since children of this age might need to go somewhat frequently. As he gets older, he will want more and more to imitate the people around him. Through his observations and your conversations with him, he will naturally recognize that the bathroom is where you use the toilet (just as the kitchen or dining room is where you eat and the bedroom is where you sleep).

Q. "I can only practice EC part-time. Won't this be confusing to the baby?"

A. Many parents erroneously believe that EC needs to be an all-or-nothing endeavor. This is absolutely not the case! Your baby can be EC'ed part-time, and she can go between a diaper and a potty just as a baby can learn to go between the breast and a bottle.

WHEN YOU ARE NOT ABLE TO BE WITH YOUR EC'ED BABY

When some people first hear about elimination communication, they think it is an impossible, labor-intensive practice, mostly involving the baby's mother, which would keep her from ever going out on her own without the baby. In fact, it may appear to them to be something reserved just for stay-at-home moms who have no other children to care for and few other responsibilities.

Indeed, a close and responsive relationship between parent and child is essential to EC, and having the time to spend with your child makes it easier to connect with him. Yet this doesn't mean that EC excludes anyone who spends time away from his or her child. Many working moms and dads practice EC, just as many working moms and dads conventionally toilet train their older children.

For parents who need to be routinely separated from their babies, EC is actually a wonderful way to make the times that you do have together a meaningful bonding experience and provides yet another way to really get to know your preverbal child. A woman at our DiaperFreeBaby meeting once noticed that her daughter was going through a phase in which she enjoyed going to the potty with her father more than she did with her mother, even though her mother was the parent at home with the child. We figured that perhaps the baby preferred the father to take her because she didn't see him as often.

As EC guru Laurie Boucke, author of *Infant Potty Training* says, elimination communication is one wonderful way that a parent who is not around all the time can bond with his or her child. It's especially gratifying for fathers. "Fathers can't breast-feed, but they can help at the other end," she says. This is one way to participate in child care in a concrete, meaningful way. The same goes for other relatives or adults who may be involved in the child's life on a regular basis, such as caregivers or grandparents. In fact, you'd be surprised how many grandparents are on board with EC, since, naturally, the concept of putting an infant on the potty was much more common some generations ago!

No matter what, if your baby is in the care of other people while you are working, EC provides another possible way for your child to gradually understand that other caring, loving people in his life will be able to help meet his needs.

Sometimes, fathers, mothers, or other adults in the child's life may not feel confident about practicing EC with a baby this young. They may not feel able to connect with the baby in this way, and they'd rather just use a diaper when they're caring for him. That's okay too, of course. In the next stage or two of their baby's life, they will probably feel more enthusiastic and confident as their child takes even more initiative for himself. For now, you, as the parent practicing EC, can always enlist the help and support of those hesitant others in different ways. My husband, for example, was always proud of his cleanup duties!

Parents Speak About Others EC'ing Their Baby:

I work, and Dorian's grandparents, uncles, and aunts all EC with him.

—DIANA, MOM TO DORIAN, 7 MONTHS

I asked about EC as part of the interview process when looking for caregivers for my daughters. I wanted a caregiver who would develop her own EC relationship with my children. We've had three caregivers and they have all EC'ed my daughters. So have my husband, my mom, and my dad.

—KEILA, MOM TO JANE, 27 MONTHS,
AND HELEN, 8 MONTHS

EC is a pretty amazing experience to be a part of. For a year and a half, I've been EC'ing these two girls I babysit. I think it's cool because it makes you really pay attention, and I believe it brings you very close to the kids. It's nice to be able to EC on the go because instead of just letting them sit and suffer, you can pull over and have a potty ready for them. It's nicer for them and quieter for you. I feel like we're making a special connection and sharing lots of laughs. I love to make funny faces, read books, or tickle their feet while they're on the potty. Sometimes people around me laugh, but I explain that even if we do miss, when I get it right and you see the happiness on their face, it feels really good.

—KAYLA, BABYSITTER TO JANE, 27 MONTHS, AND HELEN, 8 MONTHS.

I'm a pediatrician, and Betsy was my first child. Our nanny had had over ten years of direct child-care experience. When we told her that we had gotten a potty for Betsy and that she had pooped on it, our nanny thought we were nuts. She said Betsy would regress and that she would have problems later. We told her it was fine with us if she handled toileting however she was comfortable and continued to use diapers on Betsy. But after Betsy had been using the potty with us for three or four months, she really started to express her preference to poop on the potty. One day, when I got home, our nanny told me with amazement and some amusement that Betsy had been scooting along the floor fussing and turning red, and so the nanny had finally put her on the potty, whereupon she immediately pooped and was happy! After that, the nanny was on board with using the potty, and we gave her one to take to her house for when Betsy visited there. Interestingly, months before our nanny accepted using the potty with Betsy, we had a premed student babysit a few times in the evenings whose daytime job was working as a program aide with children with multiple disabilities. We told her what signals to expect and she was happy to try EC with Betsy. She had a lot of success with it even the first few times she sat with her.

—EMILY, MOM TO BETSY, 2

My wife and I both work full-time, and I would suggest EC to anyone. What I like about this method is that Felix doesn't have to sit in his own waste and that he learned from day one that his waste belongs in the toilet and not in his pants. Although it's pressing at times, I do enjoy sitting in front of him while he sits on the toilet. At the end of the day, I am glad I am spending this time with him. It is very easy to let the other parent take care of the baby and say that you will spend time with your children later. EC means I spend time with Felix, because when he needs to go, he needs to go!

—PRAVEEN, DAD TO FELIX, 17 MONTHS

MULTITASKING: EC FOR THE BUSY PARENT

You may wonder if EC is for you when it seems like your life as a parent is busy, busy, busy. How can you possibly stay alert to a child's subtle elimination signals, all the while working, taking care of household tasks, and possibly raising other children as well?

Again, as with everything, it's a question of balance. If EC resonates with you, then I can assure you that once you invest a little bit of time at the beginning to learn your child's signals and patterns, then it is not going to be overwhelming later on. And besides, as my friend Laura points out, being more in tune with your child will pay off in so many other ways by making your overall relationship more harmonious!

If EC does feel overwhelming for any reason, then you'd benefit from stepping back and seeing how EC fits into your life. You have to figure out what amount of EC is right for you. Each of the "tracks" in this book (full-time, part-time, and occasional EC) offer options that are right for your family if they fit with your lifestyle, and of course you can mix and match techniques and tips as necessary. You can start at a slow and gradual pace, see how it goes for you and your baby, and expand if it feels right. You can also take a step back if things get rough. I did this myself, scaling back to practicing EC maybe once (that is one catch, just one!) a week when we felt overwhelmed by my son's health condition when he was two to four months old. Just remember, you can always keep your baby in a diaper at times when you know life will be particularly busy. You can also anticipate those times when you'll be busy and plan accordingly. For instance, offer your baby a pottytunity right before you start to make dinner if things tend to get hectic then.

If you have older children to care for, keep in mind that EC is just another form of baby care, like changing or feeding a baby. Your older children will enjoy being involved by helping to bring the potty to you, helping support the baby on the potty, or helping to entertain the baby. I recall many times my older son would let me know that the baby had to go to the bathroom when I wasn't being attentive. We even have the cutest scene captured on video: Benjamin, not much more than a baby himself at age two, letting me know that Daniel was touching the potty and that he needed to go to the bathroom. They can actually help your baby see how normal it is to use a toilet. Babies learn so much watching their siblings use the toilet, and your older child will probably feel proud of the skills he's able to demonstrate for your baby.

Parents Speak About Siblings and EC:

The baby is always looking to her big sister, Grace, sometimes even more than she looks to my husband and me. When she sees Grace using the toilet, she wants to use it too. And Grace has also been aware of Eve's elimination and will let us know if she has to go potty. EC doesn't detract from our relationship with our older child but is instead something we all do together.

—ERIN, MOM TO GRACE, 4, AND EVE, 7 MONTHS

Jane really does help a lot with her sister when it comes to EC. Sometimes she made me feel silly for not recognizing her sister's cue.

—KEILA, MOM TO JANE, 27 MONTHS
AND HELEN, 8 MONTHS

To make EC a fun family thing, I taught my older son the ASL sign for "toilet" and asked him to make the sign for his baby sister when he thought she wanted to go. And when she got a bit older, she always wanted to pee when her brother did.

—LISA, MOM TO KAI, 3, AND NOE, 2

My preteen stepdaughters potty Ben when they visit in the summers and at Christmastime. The younger one is so in tune with him that she just knows when Ben has to go.

—GIGI, MOM TO BEN, 18 MONTHS

When people find out I have five kids they can't imagine how I've been able to EC, but I've found it to fit easily into our lives. There are plenty of opportunities for the older kids to help out. The oldest, a teenager, is able to take Jack to the toilet or potty. My six-year-old has experienced intuitive "phantom" pees on occasion, my five-year-old loves to cue Jack, and my two-year-old, who was also EC'ed, has a particular sensitivity toward Jack's needs and loves to sing him potty songs.

Many conventionally diapered and toilet-trained children will regress into wanting to wear diapers again when a new baby is born. With our EC'ed child, there was no need for her to regress because she saw the baby using the potty and toilet just like her.

—ELIZABETH, MOM OF FIVE, INCLUDING
LILLIAN, 2, AND JACK, 8 MONTHS

Maxine definitely told me when Nathan had to go, and I always listened to her. Since she was usually playing with him when I might be doing dishes or something, she was very tuned in.

—CAREN, MOM TO MAXINE, 7, AND NATHAN, 3

If Jefferson's playing with Jason in another room, he'll call me if Jason needs to be taken to the potty. If a four-year-old can pick up on a baby's need to go, anyone can!

—KATHERINE, MOM TO JEFFERSON, 4,
AND JASON, 14 MONTHS

Even older, unrelated children can be intuitive about EC because they may not have a preconceived, culturally ingrained notion that babies can't or aren't able to use a toilet.

A nine-year-old boy whom we had just met learned what we were doing with EC. A few minutes later, he announced that Dorian had to pee, and he was right.

—DIANA, MOM TO DORIAN, 7 MONTHS

Common Question: Isn't It Messy?

Q. I am eager to try EC, but my husband and I are both wondering if we're going to have messes all over the house and on our clothing.

A. EC'ing isn't necessarily messier than full-time diapering. I lived in a home that had a lot of carpet when my boys were infants. For us, it made sense to keep true diaper-free time reserved for places where we either had hardwood floor or waterproof padding on the ground. The rest of the time, I kept the baby's bottom covered, unless he had just gone to the bathroom. At home I often let him wear just a cloth diaper or training pant, a shirt on top, and leggings on the bottom, so that he could quickly get onto a potty if need be. Since he and I were in communication about his bathroom needs and I used a diaper whenever I felt it was helpful, we rarely had messes, but if they happened, I didn't regard it as a big deal.

Just remember, you can always use a diaper as backup if it helps you feel more relaxed.

Parents Speak About Misses and Messes:

I use disposable diapers. It's hard enough being a full-time mother and a full-time career woman at the same time without having to deal with accidents too often, so I use diapers. But if he has an accident, it happens; he's only a few months old; I'm not going to freak out over that. This way is easier.

—SABA, MOM TO KENAN, 8 MONTHS OLD

EC is not all that different from diapering a baby in terms of messes. When my daughter was in diapers, lots of times I had to change all her clothes if we had blowouts because it was all over her. EC is less messy because most of the time the mess gets into the toilet. In general, with EC, I'm usually not cleaning up a mess or having to wipe one off her.

—ERIN, MOM TO GRACE, 4, AND EVE, 7 MONTHS

With EC, you'll sometimes need to clean messes. Without EC, you'll be cleaning messes all the time.

—KATHERINE, MOM TO JEFFERSON, 4,
AND JASON, 14 MONTHS

AVOIDING STRESS

Inevitably, you may be wondering if EC is stressful. And no wonder. For those unfamiliar with it, infant pottying calls to mind images of harried, stressed-out, neurotic parents hovering over their babies to whisk them off to a toilet at the smallest sign that they need to go.

By now, I hope it's become obvious to you that the actual practice of EC is far different from that image! To be sure, as with any other aspect of parenting an infant, things can feel intense at times.

But by providing you with strategies and insights from other parents who have done this, I hope that you will feel that you have lots of resources to draw upon.

It can be exhilarating to catch so many of your baby's signs and to help him use the toilet. It may happen that some parents get so caught up in the fun of this mutual communication that they feel disappointed and discouraged when they go through a spell that is less successful (as can happen when baby is teething, sick, or going through a developmental change, like learning to crawl or walk). Parents may also put pressure on themselves to catch pees even in situations where it might make more sense to just use a diaper (long car trips, for example).

Of course, many parents weather this just fine, and tell themselves that tomorrow is another day. They remind themselves that EC is about the journey—the rewarding journey of communication with your child—and not about the result (i.e., pee or poop in the potty every time). Perhaps they have the advantage of having lots of supportive people around them and rarely feel moments of self-doubt. They find the whole thing so loving and effortless that they tend not to feel any stress.

But if you find yourself feeling overwhelmed or discouraged, please remember that EC can be done very part-time, or even not at all if you want to take a break. The key is to make it about communication—the actual act of "catching" is less important than communicating and acknowledging what your child is doing. You can even just let your child experience the wonderful sensation of being free of diapers. Let him go diaper-free for a half hour, and don't worry about anything else.

Parents Speak About Those Out-of-Sync Days:

There are definitely times when I know he needs to go, but he screams when I put him on the potty because he is dealing with teething pain. I just respect where he is at that particular moment. I know sometimes he just needs to be held and comforted and can't deal with anything else, and then an hour or several hours later he's happy to be on his potty again. It really changes that quickly. On the days when his mouth is hurting a great deal I just change his diaper as soon as he wets it. He stops cueing too, but when he feels better he starts cueing again.

—DEVON, MOM TO RYLER, 6 MONTHS

When Lillian's EC'ing got challenging at around six months (when she became more mobile), I didn't know anyone else EC'ing. We just worked through it. With Jack, not only did we have our experiences with Lillian to draw from but also we had the encouragement of the DiaperFreeBaby support group. So when Jack presented some of these same challenges, I had plenty of resources to draw from for tools, tips, and support. Now I look at these challenges as the exciting next step in the EC journey.

—ELIZABETH, MOM OF FIVE, INCLUDING LILLIAN, 2,
AND JACK, 8 MONTHS

His signals change often, and sometimes he doesn't signal at all, but our consistent success with communication leaves me awestruck at times. That isn't to say I don't have my frustrations and lapses. But so do parents of diapered babies.

—SARABETH, MOM TO BEN, 8 MONTHS

When confronted with a bump along the road of EC, it can seem like all too much work. Anything worth doing probably has some challenges along the way. Diaper changing involves plenty of them! Having a commitment to the basic premises of EC and maintaining a flexible attitude are the best ways to find solutions to common situations when babies and parents become out of harmony.

—RACHEL, MOM TO ISAIAH, 6, AND SIMON, 3

STAYING THE COURSE

If you find yourself having doubts about why you are doing this, just remember that EC'ed babies have the opportunity to experience the independence of really understanding their bodies and being able to communicate with you about them. This is an amazing gift in your relationship. Remind yourself of how many fewer diapers you are going through now and how much sooner you might be able to stop using them for good. These are just a few of the many reasons why so many families find EC to be immensely rewarding.

Here are a few inspiring thoughts from EC'ing parents:

There was a time when I had to remind myself to take EC lightly and not to be too attached to her going in the potty. Since then I've really tried to respect not only her resistance to going if she's having a rough day, but also my own resistance to not staying on top of her patterns. There are some days that are just not meant to be full-time EC days. The point is not to potty-train your baby, but to communicate with her.

—LARA, MOM TO RUBY, 12 MONTHS

I would say if you want to try EC but are hesitant, give it a trial period. I was hesitant at first too. I thought it might be too hard to do with so many kids, or too time-consuming and that my other responsibilities would suffer. I also wondered if it might be too much pressure on me or the baby. But I decided to give EC two weeks, during which time I would really give my best effort to tune in to my son's signals, make his needs top priority, and see how it went. If he didn't like it or either of us got stressed out, we could always just stop. I found that my son really enjoyed it, and I did too. The more you consciously relax and don't stress about EC, the better it goes.

—KATHRYN, MOM TO FIVE CHILDREN, INCLUDING T. C., 3

For those who are interested but hesitant, I'd say give it a try. We started very slowly. Most parents have a sense for when their baby needs to pee, especially the first morning pee of the day. If you know when they have to go, why not sit them on a potty and see if they'll respond? Make a cue sound every time you notice them peeing, and continue taking them for that first morning pee (or any pee you know is coming).

—SARAH, MOM TO WALLY, 19 MONTHS

I feel that with part-time EC, my goal to reduce environmental waste was accomplished as best I could. If you knew you could do something that wouldn't use up so many resources and didn't take up much of your time, then why wouldn't you do it?

—ANGELINE, MOM TO ANNA, 12 MONTHS

EC can be very, very easy. If you can offer the potty only once a day, or only after a diaper change, do that, and feel good that you are doing something. I think that EC'ing even occasionally has a lot of advantages over not EC'ing at all. I believe that the only way you can go wrong is to put too much pressure on yourself. Be kind to yourself, and if you have to make compromises, make them. Whatever works for you is right. Remember that babies are very, very smart (usually much smarter than you give them credit for) and also very forgiving. They will keep communicating as long as you are listening, even if you don't catch a single pee. What matters is that you are paying attention.

—DIANA, MOM TO DORIAN, 7 MONTHS

In the next chapter, we move on to EC'ing with your newly mobile baby and the joys of EC'ing a child on the brink of toddlerhood!

6.

The Joys of EC'ing Your Mobile Baby

Your little one has come so far in so little time. Just a few months ago, she was content to lie quietly in your arms; now she explores every nook and cranny of your home, delighting in her newfound independence. Whether or not she's close to walking, she's just about as mobile as a baby can be, and her abilities to communicate with you have expanded in many ways. Your baby is so excited by all these new developmental changes, and it's exciting for you, too, to watch her personality emerging.

You're going to want to think of new ways to make EC'ing meaningful for your baby as her interests expand. Late infancy brings new joys to the EC'ing family, as your baby learns even more ways to take the initiative with EC, but it also brings with it certain challenges. Don't worry—we'll be covering them in this chapter and telling you some favorite parent-tested solutions.

GETTING STARTED

Some of you will be coming to EC for the first time with a baby in late infancy, while others of you may have gotten started at an earlier stage. If you haven't yet tried EC with your baby, it's important to realize that your child is more conditioned by now to going in his diapers, and you'll need a slightly different approach. At this point, your baby may have tuned out of the sensation of elimination to some degree, if not completely. However, it's not difficult to help reacquaint him with his bodily awareness. Starting EC at this stage involves a simple three-step process: letting him experience wetness, helping him learn to make associations, then guiding him to eliminate in a potty or toilet. Each of these steps will be important to you whether you are practicing full-time, part-time, or occasional EC, but you'll want to follow the pace that feels right to you.

Experiencing Wetness

The first and most important step is to let your baby experience the feeling of being wet. This is for two reasons: so that your baby relearns the sensation of eliminating and correlates that with using the right muscles to release his pee, and so that you develop an awareness of his patterns. I know your baby is most likely mobile and that you may have carpeting or rugs in the home. Nevertheless, the quickest and most effective way to get your baby to recognize the pee sensation is to take him out of diapers completely.

This doesn't mean all day long, though, nor does it mean resigning yourself to letting your baby pee all over the house! Consider the most appropriate way to do this so that it fits your family and lifestyle. If the weather is warm, you can just leave your baby diaperless whenever you're outside. If you're indoors most of the time and it's not viable to have a diaper-free baby in the house, you can choose certain periods of the day to focus on EC and keep your baby diaperless only at those times. Before and after your baby has had a bath are times that work well, as do the periods before and after diaper changes. You may want to try out a diaper-free period for thirty minutes in the evening. You can always keep diaper-free time limited to a certain location in the house if you are concerned about a possible mess.

You may find that your baby does not initially eliminate without wearing a diaper. This is because he has been so conditioned to using the diaper as a toilet that he is waiting for you to put his diaper back on. This is actually a sign that he has the ability to control his bladder for at least a short period of time until he is in what he has learned is an "appropriate" situation to eliminate. Eventually, of course, he will have to eliminate, and making sure he has enough to drink can help ensure that he has the experience of being able to feel his own pee.

The same goes for bowel movements. Your baby probably displays more obvious cues when making a bowel movement than when he pees, so I've mostly concentrated on the latter here. Most parents, EC'ing or not, can tell when their baby is about to poop. But whether your baby is peeing or pooping, all your observations will provide crucial information about your baby's patterns. Once you know these patterns, you can determine optimal times to try actually positioning your baby on the potty or toilet. For instance, it is very common for babies to pee after awakening or at a certain amount of time after eating or drinking. They may also go more often during the morning and less frequently during the afternoon.

If you have been using disposable diapers rather than going totally diaperless, you can now try putting your baby in cloth diapers (preferably without a cover) or in training pants. This is almost like a "bridge" between being fully diapered and going diaper-free, and it can be an optimal choice for both parent and child when first starting out in late infancy. Using cloth diapers or training pants so your baby can feel wetness (and you can tell when she's peed) is really most crucial during this ramp-up learning stage; it doesn't mean you will never be able to use disposables again. In fact, you can use cloth for just the hour or so a day that you've designated for EC and continue to keep your baby in disposables the rest of the time. Even for that one hour or so, being in cloth will provide your baby the opportunity to experience the feeling of wetness and to know when she has gone to the bathroom, unlike in a disposable.

If your child is already using cloth diapers most of the time, your next step would be to take the cover off if possible. The difference may not be as large to her—in fact, it will feel pretty much the same—but it will make a big difference for you. You will be able to tell right away that your baby is wet. This is really crucial for teaching you her patterns and for teaching her the next step, which is to make associations between your cues and the feeling of going to the bathroom.

Parents Speak About Awareness:

Hannah, who has been EC'ed from birth, is mostly in underwear but also wears pull-ups from time to time. When she's in pull-ups, I've seen her tilt to one side and scoot and tilt again and scoot because she's very conscious that she's peed in one and is trying to get away from it. I'm so glad that she has enough consciousness of what she is doing that she tries to get away from the wetness!

—MELINDA, MOM TO SAMUEL, 3,
AND HANNAH, 10 MONTHS

Making Associations

Your baby may act very surprised the first time she senses her own pee. Or she may have little to no reaction at all. It could take several repeated pees until your child appears to know what's going on. Keep in mind that even EC'ed babies will have many times when they appear to have no reaction to having a miss. Other babies will start to crawl away and come to get you when they pee in their diaper (or make a puddle on the floor!). The most common scenario is for babies to demonstrate a bit of both—sometimes appearing hyperaware of their own elimination, other times (perhaps when distracted by something else, or when experiencing a developmental spurt, teething, new toys, etc.) not noticing at all.

In any case, as soon as *you* notice she's going to or has gone to the bathroom, cue her. Do you remember how to cue from previous chapters? If not, let's go over it again. When you hold the baby in position or place her on the potty or toilet, you make a cue sound (many EC'ers like the *"psss"* sound), and if you do this at a time when you are able to catch a pee, baby will soon start to associate that sound with peeing. If her bladder is full, she will likely pee when you make that sound in the future.

It's also a great idea to have an open-door policy when you yourself are using the bathroom. Let your baby see that you go to the bathroom too, and that you do it in a toilet. "Cue" yourself as you're doing it and keep up a conversation with your baby about why you are doing this. If you haven't already done so, teach her the American Sign Language sign for "toilet," and use that sign liberally when you are going to the bathroom. Your baby's at an age when all these conversations are going to have an accumulated impact, even if you don't think she seems to be getting anything out of them right now. And finally, showing her that you use a toilet to go to the bathroom will lead naturally to the next step, which is to teach her where to pee and poop.

Learning Where to Eliminate

You will want to introduce the potty and/or toilet (with seat insert) at this stage. Bowls and other portable containers still have their place, but with a baby this much older and bigger than a newborn, it really makes sense to use a potty right from the start. Some people like to let their child sit on the potty fully clothed for a few days before trying it diaper-free. Others find that it works well for them to start right away with naked time on the potty.

It's not at all uncommon for babies to want to play with the potty, especially if you are using a potty that has a lid. (That's why I like the Baby Bjorn Little Potty; with no removable bowl or lid, it's less distracting.) Be relaxed about this; as with any new object in the house, your child is going to be interested and want to spend some time exploring it, but you also want her to learn that it's for elimination. At some point, the potty will be commonplace to your baby, and then you will find it actually serves as a useful cue: many mobile babies will crawl over to a potty and even start patting it, playing with it, or trying to sit on it as a sign that they need to go to the bathroom!

The challenge at this age is keeping baby interested enough to sit on the potty without coercing him to stay there. Your baby does need to sit for a minute to be able to relax his muscles and release his

Hannah, ten months

bladder. You can help him to relax at these times—quite a few parents have special toys or books or songs just for potty time. If your baby is on a potty, he will probably be so fascinated by his ability to get on and off it by himself that he will want to practice this skill over and over, rather than sit still on the potty. This is another reason why some parents start using a toilet insert at this age—if baby is happily sitting on a toilet insert and is entertained by toys or books, it

Older babies can sit alone on the toilet with a seat reducer, but stay nearby for safety's sake.

won't even occur to him to try to get off the toilet by himself, since it's way beyond what he's physically capable of. Thus, he will turn his attention to other things and will be able to sit there long enough to go to the bathroom. Be sure to stay close by for safety's sake. He's not big enough to sit on the toilet without supervision. If you've read his timing and signals well, he will probably go to the bathroom within one or two minutes. Take him off if he seems fussy or distressed and entertainment doesn't distract him; you don't want him to create a negative association with the toilet or potty. But if you're sitting there and it's bonding time for him, he may really enjoy hanging out on the toilet, especially if you are enthusiastic and positive.

How Parents Started EC with Their Older Babies:

I started when my son was around eleven months old. I put him on the potty clothed, then I tried positioning him without a diaper, and he was happy staying on it but wouldn't go. I tried timing too (first thing in the morning and right after naps), but no luck. Then I did a mostly bare-bottomed weekend, to get a sense of his timing and signals. It seemed to help him understand his elimination functions, because after that he generally started going in the potty after waking up in the morning, after naps, and at a couple other times during the day.

—JULIE, MOM TO BEN, 14 MONTHS

I used to be a preschool teacher and saw many potty-training methods that I would never want to use with anyone. People see so many preschool bladder and bowel issues as normal when in reality they are a result of improper potty training. When we first heard of EC, it just made so much sense. We started when Katie was about ten months old. We bought a Baby Bjorn Little Potty and started part-time. We also taught baby signs to Katie so that she knew the sign for potty before we even started EC. Most of the time, she used the sign for potty as a cue for when she had to go. Sometimes she'd grab at herself in the beginning. By eleven, nearly twelve, months she was walking and would just go to the potty herself.

—KELLY, MOM TO KATHLEEN, 2

I gave my son lots of naked time since he was a newborn, but I didn't try EC at first. By nine months, I knew his patterns and signals pretty well, and I just couldn't keep ignoring them and letting him pee in his diapers. Because I knew he'd pee ten minutes after waking up, I started EC'ing at that time and had success right away. We added pees after naps the next week, and then went for all pees. We only practiced EC at home in the beginning. After we were more comfortable with the process, I'd take him to potty while out. Eventually I stopped using backup diapers at all.

—SARAH, MOM TO WALLY, 19 MONTHS

We started with Samuel at eight months. It was easy in a lot of ways and just got better and better. Practicing EC really made me regret the days when I used to sit there and wait while

Samuel pooped in a disposable. Starting at eight months, I thought it might be hard, but it wasn't. We only had about three poop misses after we started EC'ing.

—MELINDA, MOM TO SAMUEL, 3,
AND HANNAH, 10 MONTHS

If Nothing Seems to Be Working

If you have tried all three steps and your baby still doesn't seem to be getting the hang of releasing pee or poop into the potty or toilet, or if he doesn't even want to sit on the potty, try taking a few steps back. Make it your primary goal to simply let your baby become aware of his body again. Don't think about the toilet or potty. Give your baby as much naked time as possible and call his attention to his elimination as soon as you notice it. This will lay a foundation that you can build on when your baby reaches a new window of EC opportunity.

Parents Speak: If You Are Feeling Discouraged:

Don't underestimate the value of what you're doing! I know it's easy to wonder, "What's the point?" especially if your child is refusing to sit on the toilet or potty or won't pee in a container. When this resistance occurred with our older baby, we changed diapers frequently and simply communicated about the elimination process. Within the next few weeks or months you will almost certainly hit a window of time during which he will become more receptive to using the potty. Many families find there are several periods of high receptiveness to EC between birth and age two.

—ERIN, MOM TO EVE, 4, AND GRACE, 6 MONTHS

I have tons of misses sometimes! I try to remind myself that if I am relaxed about it, he will be more relaxed, and that it will go more smoothly. I also tell myself that it is a gradual process just like learning to do anything else (to eat, walk, get dressed, etc.).

—ILANA, MOM TO LIAM, 9 MONTHS

We've had out-of-sync days and occasional refusals to potty and then a miss a few minutes later. We just change and move on. We try to remember that these are great opportunities to communicate and that there will be many more changes later on. When there is a real pattern of misses, I've tried to focus on my son more and get reconnected by spending time "with" him and not just "near" him.

—GIGI, MOM TO BEN, 18 MONTHS

Troubleshooting: Common Issues, Simple Solutions

Issue: Your baby doesn't seem aware of her own elimination

Try: Increasing diaper-free or training-pants time. A short-term investment in diaper-free time can have a big impact on your baby's awareness.

Issue: Your baby doesn't want to sit on the potty at all

Try: Seeing if he would be amenable to another potty or a potty in a different location. Laurie Boucke also recommends keeping the potty warm with a soft potty cover. If that doesn't seem to do the trick, try leaving the potty for now and coming back to it in a few weeks. In the meantime, talk about the potty, have an open-door policy when you are going to the bathroom, cue stuffed animals on the potty, and, if your child shows interest, encourage him to pee somewhere else when cued (outdoors, standing up over a loose diaper or a bowl, or even in the bathtub). That way he will at least begin to develop an association between cueing and releasing his muscles to eliminate. When you're ready to introduce the potty again, encourage him to sit on the potty (clothed or with his diaper on if it seems that would help).

Issue: Your child is peeing very frequently with no discernible patterns

Try: Giving yourself permission to catch just some of the pees. Communicate about his other pees as much as you can. Avoid stress—many EC'ing parents with frequent pees find it works best to scale back. Check your child's diet to see if he is eating anything that could have diuretic effects (such as melon), or if he could be experiencing a food allergy, especially if he's not usually urinating this frequently. Constipation can also cause frequent peeing and/or dribbling.

Issue: You're having a lot of misses in a row

Try: Backing up. Use the "three-miss rule": three misses and back in a diaper, which alleviates any frustration you might feel about misses or messes. You can start over the next day (or whenever you feel ready to). Sometimes starting over completely—starting slowly with one usually reliable catch of the day (like morning or after a nap), then building on that over the next few days, can work well. Don't abandon EC completely, though. Remain relaxed, but keep it up.

Issue: Your child holds it on the potty, but pees right after getting off

Try: Helping him relax while on the potty. Perhaps a change of scenery or toys is what he needs. He may also want to try something different (the toilet instead of a potty, for example). Do remember that holding it on the potty and then peeing right after getting off is a typical stage that even conventionally toilet-trained children may go through. You can regard this as a positive sign that your child is starting to make a strong connection between elimination and the potty.

IF YOU'RE CONTINUING EC FROM
AN EARLIER STAGE

The steps I just outlined—developing awareness, making associations, and learning where to go to the bathroom—are intended primarily for parents who are coming to EC for the first time with their older babies, but they are also useful refreshers for those of you who have been practicing EC since the newborn or middle-infancy stages. This advice may also help you transition from one category of EC to another (part-time to full-time, for example) if you feel like this is something you are ready to do. (Remember, these categories are simply meant to be general guidelines to help you navigate this book. You are not committing to anything by choosing a certain track, and you can switch between categories as often as suits your lifestyle.)

For instance, if you are an occasional EC'er, perhaps you've only been catching bowel movements in the potty these past few months, but you are thinking of expanding to catch some pees as well. Start out with naked time, get to know your baby's patterns and let him experience the sensation of peeing, and build upon this foundation to move on to part-time or full-time EC.

If you've been following part-time EC but are interested, for example, in getting even more in sync with your baby, again, naked time (or even just putting him directly into training pants) will provide a lot of incentive for you to really get to know your baby's patterns and signals as soon as you can.

It's very easy to let things go if your baby is in a diaper. In fact, that is one of the undeniable advantages of diapers: you can focus on other things when life is very busy and you need to put off attention for a little while. Having the option of a diaper is what makes EC so manageable even though we all lead such busy lives. But by taking the next step at this stage, a whole new level of EC may open up to you, especially now that your child is probably capable of greater bladder control than he was as a newborn. You may find yourself with fewer and fewer misses, or find that you are able to take your baby out and back home in the same training pant. Your rhythms and your baby's will feel like they've fallen into sync.

At the same time, babies at this age are so excited by all their new abilities. They're starting to babble or speak. They can play for a much longer time with toys. They are starting to see that they can reach things in the house on their own because they are mobile. They're so much more communicative, which means that they will expand, by far, their ways of communicating their need to use the bathroom, through signing, vocalizing, crawling over to the potty, and more. But sometimes all these new abilities that they are so intent on practicing means that they are going to prefer to continue what they are doing rather than stop to go to the bathroom. When this happens, more often than not it's a prime time for what EC'ers call a "potty pause."

POTTY PAUSES

Every EC'ing family experiences out-of-sync moments or days. When these happen, parents wipe up and move on. It comes with the territory, and it's important not to focus on the misses.

However, if these out-of-sync days stretch out and start to last longer and longer, you could be experiencing a potty pause. This can occur at any age but seems particularly common from eight months onward, or anytime after the onset of mobility. Not every family will experience a potty pause, but if you happen to be encountering one, this information is for you.

A potty pause can be very frustrating. If it's occurring after weeks or months of smooth sailing EC, it might be difficult to accept that things are changing once again. (Remember, however, that with children, things are constantly in flux; this is a good lesson in parenting.) Keep in mind that this is an age when nursing strikes might occur; babies are highly distractible as they explore their outer world and go through developmental spurts, and a few parental adjustments can make a difference in getting things (whether that be nursing, EC, sleep, or something else) back on track.

Very often, a potty pause is a sign that your routine could benefit from some changes. Many parents report improvement if they change where the potty is located, switch to a toilet insert, bring new toys for baby to play with on the potty, or try new activities with baby while she's on the potty, such as songs or finger plays. Also, while you may previously have been matter-of-fact about your baby going to the bathroom, this is a stage when it can actually be helpful to ham it up a little. Showing your glee when your child goes to the bathroom can make a real difference in her interest in sitting on the potty.

Potty pauses are also a sign that your baby wants to take more initiative for himself. He is becoming so independent now that this is normal and should be welcomed as an important part of his development. It's the beginning of a stage in which you are going to work together with your baby to address his needs (not just EC) in much more tangible ways. The challenge is to figure out ways to accommodate and encourage his growing independence while gently guiding him.

Your baby might enjoy being able to choose between two potties, for example, or to choose which room to use. It goes without saying that having a potty that you can bring right to your child as he's playing will help as well. Some babies this age will start to signal you after they've gone to the bathroom. This is a terrific sign that they are making some connection with their bodily awareness and are also honing their abilities to convey this to you. If that's something you find your baby doing, do change him when he lets you know his diaper is wet or dirty.

It's also very common to have brief potty pauses when your child is going through a developmental spurt such as learning to crawl, walk, or talk. Teething and illness commonly disrupt sleeping or eating patterns, and your child's elimination is not immune, either.

And sometimes, babies can have what appear to be potty pauses but technically aren't, since they are very aware of their elimination and are choosing where to go to the bathroom. Ruby, daughter of my friend Lara, went through a phase where she chose not to use an actual potty as much as she used to when she was in midinfancy. Instead, she would head to a little chair (not a potty chair!) whenever she had to pee. Because she was so consistent and so obviously in touch with her body, this was different from a potty pause. Lara was great in supporting Ruby to maintain this awareness; she waterproofed the chair and kept communicating with her during this phase. The fact that Ruby was going to the chair of her own initiative whenever she needed to pee was actually an early manifestation of what many EC'ed toddlers often do: take themselves to the bathroom.

On occasion, it can sometimes be the case that a potty pause is a sign of a subtle power struggle between you and your child. Although it is a maxim of EC to stay as relaxed as possible, I know it's not always easy. Even the most easygoing parents report occasional frustration or expectations with EC, just as any parent would over other parenting issues such as eating or sleeping or even diaper changes. And when that happens, your baby can sense and react to your unspoken expectations and frustrations.

Don't beat yourself up about this; it's very normal and most parents go through power struggles to some degree now and then. One of the best things you can do for both you and your baby is to step back. Scale down. Offer the potty less. Decide to try EC again the next time or the next day. Tell yourself that you're just going to catch one or two pees (rather than most of them) or even simply remain aware of one of his pees. And keep reminding yourself that EC is not about results, it is about the process of communication. Keep those channels of communication open. I like what I've heard several

EC'ers say: if your baby is reluctant to use a potty and is having misses, remind yourself that she is trying to communicate something to you! Maintain your side of the conversation—keep talking to your child about his elimination, even if it's happening in a diaper most of the time.

Many times, potty pauses are very brief, lasting only a day or two. But sometimes they can stretch out quite a bit longer, and some parents may feel like giving up and pottying their child later in a more conventional way.

Of course, this is a choice you could make. But I'd urge you to continue EC and to try a radically different method while you ride out this potty pause. Keep the potties out, but offer them less often. Continue to have an open-bathroom policy and make a big deal out of yourself using the toilet. Focus for now almost exclusively on the act of communicating with your child about his output. If you notice him going, comment on that to him: "You're peeing!" or "You just peed, let me change you so that you can be more comfortable." Your baby can go in his diaper without undermining your earlier progress; just remember to cue him when he's going. The point is to help him maintain the bodily awareness he has developed, something that most diaper-reliant babies his age no longer have.

Maintain this communication as often as you can, cue him when you are able to, continue to let him know that he can use a potty, and change him as often as you can so he doesn't get accustomed to being in a wet diaper. Continue to offer him a potty on occasion, perhaps at some reliable times (like after waking up). If need be, tell yourself that your goal for now is to simply cue your baby while he wears diapers. Or even just make it a goal to change your baby as often as you can so he doesn't stay wet.

Consciously changing the EC category you're in—from full-time to part-time or occasional EC—can also help more than you might realize. Transitioning to a less intense track makes having reduced expectations feel more acceptable. Sometimes this shift in your own thinking and mindset are enough to jump-start a more positive interaction with your baby over EC because you are more relaxed and your baby senses this. It's not a bad thing at all to change categories dramatically. In truth, many people do so at one point or another. Remember that any degree of EC is still EC, or, as my friend Lamelle says, "Some EC is better than no EC."

THINGS TO TRY IF YOUR BABY IS BORED WITH THE POTTY

- Switching from potty to toilet insert or vice versa

- Switching potties or locations; bringing potty to baby's play area

- Having baby pee in places other than a potty (bathtub, outdoors, in a cup)

- New toys

- New songs or finger plays to make potty time fun

- Pottying a doll or stuffed animal

- Getting together with other EC'ing families and letting your baby see those other babies on potties

If your baby is bored with the potty, try getting together with other EC'ing families

When Laurie Boucke encounters parents who may be experiencing a stretch of misses, she asks them to play detective and examine what's going on at home. "When these things happen, you have to look at the whole situation," she says. "There's got to be a cause, and there are many possibilities. Sometimes it's something very simple and you just have to figure out that difference." Here are some things she's observed over the years that contribute to those out-of-sync days:

- Milestones (teething, learning to crawl, walk, or talk)

- Illness or some other discomfort, such as an injury

- Baby is becoming more independent

- Baby is resisting interruptions

- Baby wants to try something different, like the big toilet, another potty, or a different location

- New baby or visitors

- Family is moving

- Marital strife

- Travel

Parents Speak About Misses and Potty Pauses:

We had a potty pause with our first child. I think it was mainly because I wasn't going with the flow enough. We just persevered, relied on timing, and adapted to changing wet pants. Being in harmony at that time was to accept that pottying was not one of his interests at all. We had to find a way to deal with it that was okay with everyone. My daughter never had a potty pause. I very much like thinking of EC as just a way to deal with elimination until the child takes over independently, nothing more and nothing less. It takes so much stress, pressure, and focus on outcome out of the process.

—BIRGIT, MOM TO JOSCH, 4, AND NELLY, 2

Remember that catching even one pee a day is progress—and it means a lot fewer diapers over time! Forget about yesterday, strive for tomorrow; start again each day. Tomorrow, catch one; the next day, try catching the wake-up and after-nursing pees, as if you were starting all over again. That's what I try to do after a bunch of misses.

—CHARNDRA, MOM TO MAVEN, 11 MONTHS

We never had potty pauses with Samuel, although we did have misses. With Hannah, it's similar. There were a few days when the color of her poop changed, probably from being sick. I missed about a poop a day those few days, which was a little frustrating, but I was glad to be so aware of changes occurring in my child. What a nice insight!

—MELINDA, MOM TO SAMUEL, 3,
AND HANNAH, 10 MONTHS

Each developmental milestone generally meant misses and setbacks. I really had to be conscious about taking the pressure off. If we had many misses in a day and I was frustrated or down to my last pair of pants, well, it was time for the diaper for a few hours, a day, or a few days. This never lasted long, and it usually just took some slowing down on my part to reconnect with my son again.

—EMILY, MOM TO ALEXANDER, 27 MONTHS

Liam has just started walking! He's also teething. So even though he often gets too busy to want to signal or stop to use the potty, he still does pee sometimes when offered or else he will sometimes signal me after the fact so I can change him. He'll use the potty at night, after waking, and sometimes before or after a car ride. He also prefers to use the potty outside.

—ILANA, MOM TO LIAM, 11 MONTHS

If we had misses, I tried to relax a bit and see what was distracting me. Usually misses meant that I was busy or preoccupied. We had a long time, starting at ten months, when maybe twenty-five percent of pees made it into the actual potty. Simon never out-and-out refused to go potty, although I was very creative with peeing locations and maybe that helped.

—RACHEL, MOM TO ISAIAH, 6, AND SIMON, 3

If I was home but preoccupied and missed a lot, I just put him in diapers for a while and concentrated on the few consistent pees of the day (after waking up, before bed).

—JULIE, MOM TO BEN, 14 MONTHS

We experienced a potty pause at around eight months, when Orlando had just started crawling. It felt like I was really out of touch with his elimination. I was missing a lot and felt like EC "wasn't working." I knew my feelings of failure were not helping, so I decided to just let go and observe him. I observed when he peed, said "Oh, you peed," and changed him. I made no effort to catch pees at all. Somehow it helped us get back in touch and to catch more; it helped me feel better and calmer.

—STACY, MOM TO ORLANDO, 30 MONTHS

SIGNALS

At this age, your baby may be increasing the many ways she can show you that she needs to go to the bathroom. It's important to keep in mind that these signals might change often. Moreover, sig-

Is It a Potty Pause or Something Else?

If your child suddenly has a string of misses after months of consistently using the toilet, it's natural to assume he is experiencing a potty pause. However, a little sleuthing might reveal another underlying cause.

One mom I know, Thembi, was puzzled when little Nina suddenly started having misses. As an infant, she wore underwear, signed "potty," and could go on hours-long shopping trips with no misses. Suddenly she started having a few misses here or there while at home (which Thembi took in stride), and then a few days later Thembi found she was dealing with a "never-ending trickle of pee." Nina was dribbling small quantities of pee constantly; there were drips (not puddles) on the floor, and she started peeing at night more than twice as much as just a few weeks before. After talking it over with other EC'ing parents and realizing that this was more than just potty-pause behavior, Thembi took Nina to the doctor and found out that constipation was putting pressure on Nina's bladder, causing all those dribbles and misses. Had they not been practicing EC, they probably would not have noticed that Nina was so uncomfortable. Once they addressed the constipation, the misses subsided.

nals that your baby may have used throughout infancy until now may disappear. She may use other signals instead, or she may use nothing for a while. There may be periods throughout your child's infancy when you seem to notice very few overt signals about impending elimination. Just keep in mind that all this is normal.

How Older Babies Say They Have to Go to the Bathroom

Jack's signals have changed over time. He has used the ASL toilet sign, tapped me on the shoulder, and crawled to the bathroom, but his new one is my favorite. Now he says "Bob" when he needs to go. Most people call the toilet the "John," but "Bob" works too!

—ELIZABETH, MOTHER OF FIVE INCLUDING
EC'ED LILLIAN, 2, AND JACK, 8 MONTHS

Our baby sat in a booster chair at the table when he was eight to nine months old. No matter what food or drink I'd put in front of him, he'd usually pitch it partway through the meal. This behavior continued for a long time. After we started EC when he was ten months old, I noticed that he always threw his food right when he had to pee! It was still a challenge to catch the moment and take him to pee before he threw his food, but at least we knew why he did it!

—CAREN, MOM TO MAXINE, 7, AND NATHAN, 3

At eight months, if there were no potty nearby, Nina would make a certain sound, kind of an urgent "uh, uh, uh," that let me know she needed to pee. At home, sometimes she'd crawl over to the potty, grab it, and look at us expectantly. She still makes those signs today, but she'll also try to climb on us now that she's more mobile, as if trying to get our attention, and—most exciting—for a few months she's been using the sign we taught her for potty.

—THEMBI, MOM TO NINA, 12 MONTHS

Common Times You Might Have a Miss

My friend Melinda, DiaperFreeBaby cofounder, compiled this handy little list of common times you might have a miss.

- While you are preparing meals

- When baby's siblings are requiring attention

- After baby has a nap, if she is young or if you're not right there when she wakes up

- When baby is traveling in a car seat and you can't stop for her

- When baby is in a reclined position in a stroller or bouncy seat

- Right after a miss—misses are often partial misses and baby hasn't emptied her bladder. If you don't put her on the potty she may then release more pee while being changed

- When baby is on her belly

- When others are taking care of baby

- When baby is in an Exersaucer

EC ON THE GO

If your baby is eliminating mainly in the potty at home, but you haven't really ventured out of the home to try EC, this is a really good age to consider doing so. In fact, your baby will quite possibly be more comfortable this way if she's growing more and more accustomed to the comfortable feeling of going in a toilet rather than in a diaper. Public pottying is not the hassle you might imagine it to

Clean Up Time

It's useful to have a collection of spray bottles filled with water and disinfectant or your favorite natural cleaner. Some people like to use a vinegar-water combination, whereas others prefer a commercially made cleaner (with separate ones for rugs and wooden floors). Keep these at various places around the house, along with some paper towels or a little stash of washcloths or prefolds. Also keep spray bottles handy in the car, in each bathroom, and in most rooms where the baby tends to be located (stored out of baby's reach). As long as you're prepared, wiping up a little miss will be simple. I have even found that plain old liquid or dishwashing soap or laundry detergent is ideal for cleaning up any misses that may occur on rugs or carpets. Blot up the stain, dilute with water, apply soap, rub in well, and then rinse with clean water. One product that many families list as their favorite is Bac-Out by Bi-O-Kleen. This natural stain remover works well on any textile, such as clothing, towels, diapers, and rugs. (Be sure to follow the directions and check for colorfastness first.)

be. Things are different from when she was a newborn. She is older and may have developed the sort of control that will allow you a little more time to find a bathroom for her. Sometimes, "preemptive pottying"—taking your baby to the bathroom when you happen to be near a restroom, if you know you won't be near one later on—is helpful in keeping your child comfortable and dry.

The following strategies for applying EC on the go are similar to those mentioned in previous chapters, except that you now have the additional benefit of being able to use a toilet with a child who is much older. Here are the main tips to remember:

- Scout out bathrooms when you go to a new place

- If traveling, take along a potty and/or toilet insert that your baby is comfortable with, along with any bowls that you might find helpful

- Offer opportunities before leaving the house, after coming back home, and if you happen to be near a bathroom or even happen to be using one yourself

- Cue baby to go in a diaper too if necessary

- Keep a potty in the car

We offered pottytunities whenever we thought Felix might need to go while we were out, and my notes from his infancy are littered with comments about places where he went (the pediatrician's, the mall, certain restaurants, friends' houses, etc.) When Felix was ten months old, we took a three-day trip with plane rides and a hotel stay, and we managed the whole thing with only three pee misses. In fact, we seemed to fare better with EC while out, since we were more alert and tuned in, and Felix was carried in a wrap.

—KAREN, MOM TO FELIX, 17 MONTHS

We were traveling home from somewhere, and Nathan was uncomfortable in his car seat. I tried music, talking, toys . . . all the things that I thought might help. He was just starting to babble and said "Baboo" (his word for bowel movements). I pulled over to the side of the road and set him on the potty in the back of the car. He had a bowel movement right away, and I was so glad I could respond to his discomfort. If I hadn't known, we would have listened to him screaming all the way home.

—CAREN, MOM TO MAXINE, 7, AND NATHAN, 3

Is EC Convenient?
One Parent Speaks

Convenience is not a dirty word. It's extremely important for a parent to feel peaceful and relaxed, and searching for simplicity and convenience is an excellent way to accomplish that. There's no objective definition of convenience either. It's whatever works for you. Some people feel diapers are convenient, and some people feel that not using diapers is convenient.

We practiced EC from birth, but when I went back to work a few months after our daughter was born, we went back to diapering and did not try to catch every pee. That was the choice that worked for our needs at the time. We'd still catch the occasional pee and a good number of poops (which really does save time—just flush and snap and you're done). So we were still following a hybrid version of EC.

In practice, EC will probably take more mental effort during the first few months than diapering. But at some point there is going to be a crossing point where EC starts taking less mental effort and far less time and expense than diapering. And then eventually you'll have a toddler who might be using a potty a year or even two or three years before she might have without EC. That is a source of daily celebration.

—MATTEO, DAD TO CARLY, 5, AND JASMINE, 3

EC'ING WITH OTHER PEOPLE

If your baby spends time in the care of other people, this is an ideal age for your baby to begin being EC'ed by other people as well. Teach your caregivers that your baby has certain patterns, and ask them if they can possibly potty your baby once or twice while they are watching her. You can also tell them just to offer your baby a pottytunity when the diaper is off during a diaper change.

If caregivers are resistant to the idea of taking your child to the potty, you can ask them to consider doing it if your baby makes any overt gestures indicating her need to use a toilet (i.e., she starts playing with the potty, signing, etc.). If they are reluctant even to do that, then encourage them to, at the very least, communicate with your child and cue her about what she is doing if they happen to notice.

Late infancy does happen to be a prime age for stranger anxiety, and your baby may associate EC so much with bonding time with you that it takes some time to be receptive to someone else's cues. On the other hand, babies this age are so interested in the world around them that they may actually exhibit a strong preference for new people to play with or assist them in going potty. Many children even go through phases where they will prefer one parent rather than the other for pottying and other needs. This is normal. Be sure to ask your caregiver to remain open to your baby's cues.

Here are some of the most rewarding parts about EC'ing your vibrant older baby. Read this for inspiration and support!

Parents Discuss What They Love About EC at This Stage:

> At nine months old, Alexander flew with me alone from Boston to Hawaii. Once in Hawaii, my son learned the joys of going naked in the warmth and peeing standing up. I have fond memories of a little pudgy naked guy crawling to a lawn chair, pulling himself up, and peeing while gazing at the Maui surf!
>
> —ERINN, MOM TO ALEXANDER, 2

> Some people think we've made it up and don't believe that Nina is out of diapers. Most people are just amazed and tell us what a

great job we're doing—but I really believe that the decision to use the potty was more Nina's than ours. We enable it, but she makes it work.

—THEMBI, MOM TO NINA, 12 MONTHS

What's great about EC is that it welcomes Hannah into a common practice with other people—"Your turn to use the toilet, Hannah"—instead of excluding her from the bathroom experience. It really is a way to involve Hannah in her own care and help her to learn healthy body habits while building communication and trust between us. Plus, EC is fun because it's better than going in a diaper!

—MELINDA, MOM TO SAMUEL, 3,
AND HANNAH, 10 MONTHS

What my babies and I got out of doing EC was a very well developed communication. It was only on very rare occasions that I didn't know what my baby needed. I believe that for us, this ability to understand what our babies were conveying to us was trained and refined by the process of EC.

—BIRGIT, MOM TO JOSCH, 4, AND NELLY, 2

Our journey to EC began with my aversion to disposable diapers. But cloth diapers weren't satisfactory to me either. Finally, we pretty much stopped using any diapers at all. At five months things changed drastically—Yunna started signaling very actively, and our catch rate went up significantly. Although we've had some setbacks (like when teething), if we had misses, we would just laugh them off. Now, at eleven months, we usually have no more than one to two misses a day, with some days being completely dry.

—JULIA, MOM TO YUNNA, 11 MONTHS

I know my son in ways I didn't think were possible until he was much older. You know how people say that once their toddlers start talking they're like a little person? I already have that, and have had it since I learned to tune in and to be present with my baby.

—GIGI, MOM TO BEN, 18 MONTHS

It probably seems that time has flown incredibly fast—your baby is quickly moving toward toddlerhood! Life will change for you in so many ways. The communication skills you've fostered through the practice of EC will continue to benefit you greatly as you move on to this next, exciting stage.

7.

EC'ing Your Toddler

It's one of the breathtaking privileges of parenthood to watch your little baby become a toddler. It's never more apparent than now what kind of little person she's going to be, and her antics are so much fun to watch! Children of this age are enthusiastic, love to imitate adults, and are often willing to participate in anything and everything with you. They take delight in discovering new things in the world around them. Learning to walk makes the world particularly accessible to them in a new way. Understanding and working with your child's developmental stage will help you guide him in staying on the EC track while acknowledging his need to explore and play. Luckily, as many parents have found, the two are not mutually incompatible!

BEGINNING EC WITH A TODDLER

If you are beginning EC for the first time with your toddler, your strategies are going to differ from those used by parents who are EC'ing a newborn or six-month-old child. Your child is likely no longer very much in touch with his bodily awareness if he's been diapered throughout infancy. But he is still so young, and toddlers have certain traits (like being able to walk and talk) that make EC'ing flow particularly well at this age, so don't be discouraged! Your approach will be very similar to the one described in chapter 6, because it includes the additional step of reacquainting your child with his bodily awareness. Introducing EC to your older baby or toddler is a three-step process: letting him become aware of his elimination, making associations and teaching him about cueing, and finally guiding him to eliminate in a toilet or potty.

Becoming Aware of Elimination

It's important to let your child spend some time out of diapers. You might remember my story from the beginning of this book: my first son, Benjamin, started using the potty when he was just thirteen months old. I gave him plenty of diaper-free time in those first few days to reinforce his awareness of the sensation of elimination.

In order to provide diaper-free time, you can either take your child out of diapers completely or put him in a training pant or a coverless cloth diaper. The purpose is twofold: to let him sense what it feels like to pee (he will immediately look down, and, after repeated experiences, will start to associate the pee sensation with the muscles he uses for eliminating) and to let you know what his patterns are. A common pattern is for babies and toddlers to pee soon after waking up and at a certain amount of time after drinking or eating (this varies from child to child but is often consistent for each child). It's also common for children to pee more often in the morning and less often during the afternoon. Whatever your child's particular patterns are, it is essential that you understand them. This knowledge will enable you to choose the best times to let your baby go diaper-free, as you'll soon know when you have the optimal chance of observing him eliminate. For us, morning was a good choice because I knew my son would pee often then and it would give both of us a lot of opportunities. For others, especially those who work, evenings are better because they are a great time to reconnect with your child. And remember, a diaper-free period doesn't have to last long; even fifteen or twenty minutes is fine. If you don't happen to get any output during that time, you've still gained the valuable insight that your baby doesn't tend to go at that time or that he can hold it. You can always switch diaper-free time to a different period of the day if need be.

You might occasionally get some pee on the floor, just as you would if you were providing naked time during conventional toilet training. Use a training pant or cloth diaper for nearly the same effect as total naked time if you will be bothered by this, as it's important not to get stressed about the learning process.

Making Associations

Once Benjamin started to notice he was peeing, he'd look down, exclaim, or have some sort of adorable reaction. Having been in diapers all his life, he'd never noticed what he was doing before, and this was just amazing to him. When he reacted, I'd say, "You're peeing!" and then make the cue sound (*pssss*). I even signed "toilet" at the same time for maximum effect. Thus, I was communicating to him about what he was doing in three different ways. If I noticed him starting to squat or strain, I'd also say, "You're going to poop!" (And then,

Even toddlers enjoy having their parents nearby when they're on the potty.

if I had a potty handy, I'd put it under him to catch the poop; you can also use a diaper or container.) Don't say anything in an alarming way; you just have to call their attention to what they are doing. This is making an association, responding to their reactions, and teaching them cues and signals that they can use. With Benjamin, I also noted how frequently he was going, which provided me with the information I needed to determine the most appropriate times to offer him the potty.

Using the Potty or Toilet

Once your child appears aware of the pee sensation and is starting to make a connection between peeing and cues, and once you are also developing a good awareness for when he needs to go to the bathroom, you can start to offer the potty or toilet. Keep toys or books around the potty to make the experience fun, and make it clear to your child that sitting on the potty is going to be a very special bonding time. Also be sure to make the cue sounds he has learned to associate with eliminating as you place him on the potty.

Some children may still have trouble releasing their pee or especially their poop in this new position. Be patient. If your child's trouble persists, go back to step two and simply work on his associations. At this stage, it's most important that he learn these associations and become reacquainted with his bodily awareness. There will be time enough for potties later on. Nevertheless, keep offering the potty at intervals so that he knows the opportunity is there for him if he is ready. Dumping the contents of his diaper into the toilet will also help him make the connection between elimination and the potty or toilet.

IF YOUR CHILD IS UNENTHUSIASTIC ABOUT THE POTTY

Some people find that their children are very resistant to the potty or toilet. If this is the case, again, you may wish to stay in the "association" stage for a while. It's quite common for there to be windows of time when your child is naturally eager to sit on a potty, and others when your child seems to want nothing to do with it. Keeping a potty available and introducing it every once in a while is a good way to determine if it's an appropriate time to start helping your child use the potty.

Remember to try other methods, such as offering different potties, or using Potty Bowls, or toilets with a toilet insert. Quite a few parents find that their toddlers will pee while being cued when they are outdoors or in the shower or bath. You can also offer other containers for your child to pee in, like a plastic cup or bottle.

If your child is reluctant about the potty, and you find yourself feeling frustrated, it might help you to take a look at things from your child's point of view. Consider how you would feel if suddenly you had to switch positions and eliminate in a totally different position or place than you were used to. Maybe you have even experienced this firsthand during a camping trip or other outdoor excursion. Think about it for a second: isn't it a bit hard to switch gears? This is what your child is going through. Be patient. It's normal and even healthy for the process to be gradual. Quite a few toddlers who were exclusively diapered throughout infancy will show a strong attachment to their diapers (actually asking for or waiting for a diaper before eliminating). Given that the diaper is what your child is used to, this is more than understandable. Respect this attachment while continuing to help your child redevelop his bodily awareness. Keep talking about or offering chances to use the potty. And remember—all of this is still progress! Just a short while ago, your baby appeared to have little to no awareness of his own elimination at all. How far he has come in so little time!

Parents Speak About Getting Started
EC'ing a Toddler:

I started EC when Corwin was fourteen to fifteen months old. I began by giving him diaper-free time for two hours each morning and switching to two to three cloth diapers a day. It took one week before he started to notice if he had peed on the floor; he would bring me to the area to clean it up. I also began to cue him in the tub (because he was reluctant to use the toilet) after naps. About one month after starting, he was really associating the sound "sss" with peeing, and he had also switched to using the toilet. For poops, I'd sit him on the toilet, sometimes right after he got started, and he'd happily finish off there if I gave him something fun to play with.

—HELEN, MOM TO CORWIN, 19 MONTHS

One Mother's Late-Start EC Story

Aidan had been interested in using the toilet for a while, and I had absolutely no clue how to help him. When I asked friends, their responses ranged from "It's too early" to "I used bribes." This didn't sit right with me. A music teacher who overheard him saying "toilet" said to me, "You are pushing him. He is way too young to use the toilet," even though his request was completely unprompted by anyone. Finally we went to a pediatrician's office, and when I mentioned Aidan was interested in the toilet, he dismissed me, saying, "Just ignore it. He's too young. Most boys don't use the toilet until they are at least two and a half."

The next day I was in a toy store, juggling a huge basket in a crowded line, when Aidan looked up at me and said, "Toilet." I replied, "Honey, can you please pee in your diaper?" But he looked at me again and said, "No. Toilet." Just then a woman tapped me on the shoulder. I turned, and she asked, "How old is your son?" I thought, Oh no, if another person tells me I am pushing him, I am going to belt her. I said, "He's eighteen months," and turned abruptly around. She said, "That's great. You are doing a nice job of listening to him. My son was using the toilet at that age too." Her name was Melinda, and she was a cofounder of DiaperFreeBaby.

From that encounter I learned about EC and discovered support groups we could attend. Finally I had found a way to help Aidan. The whole approach resonated with us. It was a way for me to help him in his interest to use the toilet without "training" him.

We started out part-time. We used underwear in the morning, when we have pretty relaxed, slow time and I could hang out with him and wouldn't be stressed about cleaning up any misses. Over time he stayed drier longer, until he was wearing underwear all day, both at home and out and about.

—MARIE, MOM TO AIDAN, 29 MONTHS

EC'ING BY OTHERS

As a toddler, your child will have many opportunities for others to EC her. Because she probably has so many ways to convey the need to go to the bathroom, you'll probably find that you encounter less resistance from partners, family members, caregivers, and teachers than you might have when she was an infant.

Because Betsy joined a toddler class for kids aged fifteen months to two years, nine months, the teachers realize that most of the children will start to learn toileting skills at some point while they're in the class. Also, for the kids who have not yet learned to use the toilet, the teachers are responsible for changing their diapers. They were very happy to help Betsy use the potty from a younger age. In fact, one of her teachers (who has a son in the class who is two weeks younger than Betsy) recently told me that she wished she had started using the potty early with her son as well.

—EMILY, MOM TO BETSY, 2

EC'ING YOUR ONE-YEAR-OLD: HELPING HIM TAKE THE INITIATIVE

EC'ing a one-year-old is a very different experience from EC'ing a baby. Because your child now has so much independence, he can be much more involved in the whole process. I found that my children really loved the whole toilet ritual as toddlers. They loved wiping, putting paper in the toilet, flushing, and washing hands afterward. This was all engaging to them and, most important, made them feel that they were imitating what they had observed adults doing. It was a very important process to them.

To take advantage of that innate developmental drive to imitate, you will want to accelerate your open-bathroom-door policy. Talk to your child about everything you are doing when you go to the bathroom, every step of the way. Ask other adults in the house if they are willing to do this too. (My brother let my son Benjamin go into the bathroom with him once, and he was startled and amused to find my son cueing *him* to pee!) If you have older children around who are already using the toilet, definitely involve them as well; they are probably going to be so proud of their abilities to teach your baby something. You will never again have such a fascinated audience

My son Daniel demonstrating
the ASL sign for "toilet"
(wave hand back and forth)

(until you have your next one-
year-old child!).

Children this age are able
to communicate much more
clearly than they could when
younger. At one year old, Benjamin was saying his own form
of the cue sound (*pssss*), in addition to signing "toilet" in ASL.
He could tell me that he had to go to the bathroom even though he
was not verbal yet. Thus, it is important to teach your child ways to
communicate the need to use the toilet, or else take note of his own
signals and cues and encourage him to use them. The best way is to
continue to communicate with him as actively as possible. There's no
such thing as overdoing it; talk about going to the bathroom as much
as you can when it's relevant.

Be sure to keep up your use of the ASL toilet sign. It may seem
like it takes awhile until your child gets the hang of it and starts signing it back to you, but once he does it will make things simpler for
you. You may have to educate other adults in your child's life, as well.
One mom I know, Sarah, says that because her little boy is so young,
when he signs "toilet," most people assume he's waving and respond
by saying, "Bye-bye!"

Lots of parents report that their toddlers start cueing dolls or
stuffed animals to pee. This is a wonderful sign that your child is
getting the idea, even if she's not actually using the potty a whole lot
herself! Play really speaks to young children on a level they can

understand, so get down on the floor with your child and have some fun with her stuffed animals or dolls. Have them all cue each other. Keep the idea of pottying as fun as possible!

THE PERILS OF PRAISE

By the way, I want to make one little comment about how important it is to allow this pottying experience to belong to your child and not to you or anyone else. You'll notice that throughout the book, I have encouraged you to acknowledge when your child is going to the bathroom. This is a really important part of maintaining your child's bodily awareness and cluing him in to the fact that he's going to the bathroom.

You're probably very delighted for your child—which is a really good, in fact, a wonderful, thing! Your warmth and enthusiasm make the potty process pleasant and positive for your child. But I have never told you to say "Good boy!" or "Good job!" or to offer any sort of general praise like that. I've noticed that many EC'ers avoid the use of praise or rewards because they want their children to know that this accomplishment is theirs and theirs alone. They don't want to inadvertently encourage their children to use the toilet for external validation (such as a reward or to please the parent). And just as we usually don't reward our children for eating or sleeping, going to the bathroom in the potty is another matter-of-fact process (especially if you've been doing it all your life).

That said, I am not at all saying that you should stifle your positive feelings. Acknowledging your child's accomplishment, perhaps by saying how good it must feel for her, or by expressing delight for her that she's gotten the hang of this concept, will leave the whole experience right where it belongs—with her. (By the same token, this is why it is so important to remain unemotional, matter-of-fact, and supportive if your child has a miss).

Critics of EC sometimes wonder if children will eventually

regress because they stop wanting to please the parent. The truth is, however, that with EC, from the very beginning, the emphasis is on the child achieving it for herself and no one else. Keep your comments in the realm of affirming, positive reinforcement rather than praise.

Parents Speak about Positive Reinforcement:

> Since the urge to eliminate is something that no one can control, it didn't make sense to praise or reward Neshama for having this urge and acting on it when I gave her the chance to go in the toilet. At the same time, I wanted to create a positive atmosphere around pottying. I decided to focus on the good feelings we humans experience when we eliminate. So I narrate the experience for Neshama with a positive spin: "You're going tinkle! It feels so good to tinkle; what a relief!" It's a small change in words, but I do believe words make a difference.
>
> —LAMELLE, MOM TO NESHAMA, 12 MONTHS

TROUBLESHOOTING

Q. I just don't want to go diaper-free. Is this even necessary?

A. No, going diaper-free is not necessary. Some diaper-free time does help raise your awareness and your baby's, and usually motivates parents to tune in a bit more than if baby were in a diaper, but it would be counterproductive to go without diapers if the idea stressed you out. Having a relaxed, patient attitude is paramount to EC, so it's important to do what you feel comfortable with. If you are interested in trying just a bit of diaper-free time, try what my friend Marie did: restrict diaper-free time to the kitchen or in other places that are easy to clean in case your baby has a miss. If Marie's son started to wander away, she simply put a diaper on him.

HOW TODDLERS SAY THEY HAVE TO GO TO THE BATHROOM

- Saying toilet or pee
- Looking down at legs
- Clutching self between legs
- Running toward toilet
- Pause in behavior
- Signaling or signing
- Playing with or trying to sit on potty or toilet
- Pulling off pants
- Heavy breathing or grunting
- Getting whiny or asking for attention or to nurse
- Asking to be picked up

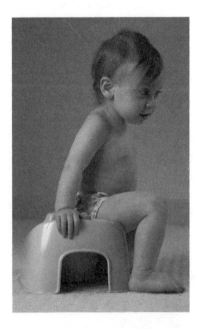

Your toddler may attempt to sit on the potty as a sign she has to go.

STRATEGIES FOR EC'ING A ONE-YEAR OLD

EC'ing a one-year-old is much simpler than EC'ing during the baby stage in some ways. The mobility which can sometimes make EC challenging also makes toddlers much more independent about using the potty. It's not uncommon to see toddlers rush to the bathroom when they feel the urge to go. Boys can now pee standing up, unlike when they were babies. This is really useful. My own experience with my sons revealed the particular merits of the standing-up stage; whenever the boys were too engrossed in their play to take a potty break, I could just let them pee, standing up, into a little bottle or cup. It was also useful if we were in a strange bathroom (at a friend's house or out in public) and my children felt shy about using a new toilet. And if you have a daughter, she can pee anywhere too, squatting into a container or bowl. This ability actually would come in handy in the event that your child has to produce a urine sample at the doctor's office!

Because toddlers are older, too, their bodies are bigger, their bladders are bigger, and they are able to go longer periods in between pees. This sort of sphincter control can come about remarkably rapidly even if one only just started EC'ing. Two weeks after my son had started using the potty, we were in the car on a highway and he suddenly signaled "toilet" to me. Although he was in a backup diaper, he didn't want to use it. I had nowhere to stop and felt very bad about it. It ended up being twenty minutes until we got home, but he waited until we arrived, then went to the bathroom happily!

If your child is still in diapers but you're having very few misses, consider taking the plunge and moving into training pants. (Disposable pull-ups are another option, but they can get expensive.) It might feel a little nerve-wracking at first, but pack a change of clothes as a backup, and see where it takes you.

Aidan had been wearing underwear at home for a while, but we were using diapers to go out. One day when we were rushing to get to the grocery store, I tried changing him out of underwear and into a diaper, but he insisted on underwear. I took a deep breath. I didn't want to discourage him and I had to start sometime, but why today! I got a bag ready with extra clothes, underwear, and plastic bags, and filled my mind with all the accidents that might occur. But he made it dry through that outing and our next one, too. One time after that, however, we had a bunch of errands to run and he consented to wearing a diaper. At our first stop, I was holding him on my hip and I felt a warm wetness; the disposable diaper had leaked. How ironic it was that we could keep underwear dry during our outings, but had an accident when he was wearing a fresh diaper! I had to laugh, and from then on, I relaxed about going out.

—MARIE, MOM TO AIDAN, 29 MONTHS

Recently I took my son, Zane (who was fourteen months at the time), to do some grocery shopping. Zane had been sleeping during the ride over but woke up when we arrived at the store. As soon as I took him out of the car seat, he made the potty sign. I wasn't sure we'd make it all the way to the bathroom (we were still far and I didn't know where the bathroom was), but I told him I'd try. I took him there, but just as we were about to go inside, someone stepped in ahead of us. We waited and got bored. Just as we started wandering away, Zane started making the sign again, so we tried again—and again someone got in line before us. I was sure he would have just given up and gone in his pants, but no; when he finally went, he happily peed!

—KAREN, MOM TO ZANE, 16 MONTHS

EC'ing a Toddler in a Public Restroom

With toddlers, sometimes a new issue with public restrooms will rear its head. Toddlers may be getting heavy for the in-arms position, but may not be willing to sit on a strange toilet. Here are some things you can do:

- Take your child into public restrooms frequently so he gets used to them

- Have your child pee in a Potty Bowl or container in the restroom

- If your child is a boy, start cueing him to pee standing up into the toilet (if he's too short, you can lift him up a few inches) or else into a little bottle or cup near the toilet (again, while standing)

- Bring along your own portable toilet seat reducer insert or a portable potty that your child is comfortable with

- Have a stash of seat covers or wipes in your bag to clean off and cover the toilet seat before your child sits down

EC AND TRAVEL

When traveling with your toddler, EC may fall into place even better—or it may not. Many parents do find that having some free time to focus on their children makes EC proceed more smoothly, but children can be thrown off course by travel, planes, time changes, new bathrooms, and so forth. Consider bringing your child's favorite toilet insert or potty along.

I also want to note that sometimes jet lag or a time change, especially if it's a considerable difference, can cause a change in your child's patterns. As his body adjusts to the new time, there can be temporary bed-wetting when there was none previously. This is normal, and you should plan for the possibility accordingly.

EC'ing Your Toddler at Night

Some of you may notice that your toddler is now dry for longer stretches (being dry for most or all of the night is not that uncommon). On the other hand, others of you may find that your child is wetting heavily at night or waking up to go to the bathroom. As I've said in previous chapters, how you choose to handle nighttime EC is up to you. Some parents prefer to diaper their babies and toddlers at night in order to prioritize long stretches of sleep, whereas other parents may keep their children in training pants or underwear and take them to the bathroom to assist them in staying dry. Some parents find that their toddlers stay dry at night if they potty them once late in the evening (several hours after their child has gone to sleep; perhaps right before you are about to go to bed). Amazingly, some children can be taken to the toilet or potty in their sleep without waking up at all (one of my sons was this way), whereas other children will wake up completely if their parents disturb them (my other son was like this!). I found that with both of my children, the period of time when I needed to assist them at night was relatively brief, since they became dry at night fairly early on, although there were periods during both of their second years when they would again need to pee at night. If your baby happens to be dry from a young age, don't be concerned if this changes from time to time throughout toddlerhood—it's normal. The EC'ing families I know have made the nighttime choices that were right for them, including: diapering their children at night until their children eventually developed the physical capacity to stay dry, assisting their children to go to the bathroom once or twice a night, or changing the diapers or underpants if they happened to notice the pants were wet and the child was not explicitly asking to be taken to the potty or toilet. You know your own child and your family priorities best. Do what feels right for you, but remain open to all possibilities. The situation will almost certainly change at some point.

I'll close this chapter with a couple of thoughts from parents just like you who are experiencing the joys of EC'ing their toddlers:

I work and have a nanny that is supportive of EC. She started putting her own daughter (now eighteen) on the potty when she was six months old. My son wears disposables overnight and for naps and outings, and Gerber training pants when we practice EC. But even when he's wearing disposables while we're out, I will try to take him to the bathroom if one is readily available. He peed in the bathroom of the Metropolitan Museum of Art a few weeks ago.

EC provides a time during the day when we can interact quietly. At this age, Ben is running around so much and doesn't spend a lot of time in-arms anymore. EC offers a nice opportunity for us to be together and interact. We play peek-a-boo, look at books, play with empty toilet paper rolls, or look in the mirror. When he goes to the bathroom we say, "Bye-bye" and flush it down the toilet.

—JULIE, MOM TO BEN, 14 MONTHS

I offer the potty after Jason's nap, and if he goes, he goes. Afterward, I put some underwear on him. I prefer underwear to diapers; after three years of diaper changing with my first child, I recognize that it's easier to change a pair of underwear than to change a diaper. Also, underwear is more likely to stay on than a diaper. With underwear, it's always apparent when he's wet. He helps with changing his underwear but kicks and screams during a diaper change.

—MARTY, DAD TO JASON, 14 MONTHS

From the age of twelve months, my daughter would specifically request certain people to take her to pee, including Mom, Dad, Grandma, a friend's parent, and especially a friend of mine who hangs out with us a lot.

—LISA, MOM TO KAI, 3,
AND NOE, 2

It really feels natural to bond while your child is peeing or pooping. I never did anything to make it especially "fun," but it was just like all those other things you do with your child, such as feeding or dressing him. I tried to engage him in a friendly way and talk to him about what was happening.

—STACY, MOM TO ORLANDO, 30 MONTHS

I have an overall, daily appreciation for how practical and simple EC can be. For instance, when we're out of the house and all the other kids have diapers on, my son just turns to me and says, "Poo-poo," and off we go to the bathroom together.

—RON, DAD TO ORLANDO, 30 MONTHS

Following EC helps us to stay in tune and connected with each other. If he were still in diapers, I would be able to get more absorbed in whatever I were doing and kind of tune him out.

Because we EC, I remain alert to his little signals. Sometimes we tickle his belly when he has trouble relaxing his bladder, and he laughs.

—SARAH, MOM TO WALLY, 19 MONTHS

8.

Final Hurdles and Graduation

You're almost there! You and your child are EC pros by now, and completely dry, miss-free, diaper-free days are just around the corner. In this chapter we'll look at some of the final hurdles you and your child might encounter as you approach the end of your EC journey. While many families move toward "graduation," or toilet independence, without a hitch, others encounter varying degrees of challenges, including potty pauses.

But don't be discouraged! Most toddler potty pauses seem to be the very final step right before graduation. And not everyone encounters this. There are so many paths to graduation, as you're about to read. Soon enough, you and your child will have your own graduation story to share.

TODDLER POTTY PAUSES

Just as in previous stages, some families might experience potty pauses of varying duration during the toddler years. It's very important to note that not all EC'ing families experience potty pauses. Although most families probably experience their share of out-of-sync days here or there, the following section is meant to provide guidance and reassurance for those rarer potty pauses that stretch out for longer periods of time. Illness, teething, travel, and visitors can all throw things off just as they can throw off sleeping or eating patterns. Also, it's developmentally normal for your child to be so immersed in her play that she won't want to stop for any interruptions, such as eating, drinking, or using the bathroom. She may also be experimenting with her own expanding abilities to see how much of the outer world she can control.

As I've mentioned before, it's important to see if changes to your routine helps your child become interested in using the bathroom again. Using different potties, switching from potty to toilet or vice versa, offering a potty in a different location, offering your child a choice of potties, changing what toys or books you have around the potty, or offering your child a sippy cup of water to help her relax enough to pee are all strategies that have helped families to move beyond these potty pauses. Each child is different, so be open to trying many different things until you figure out what works with your toddler.

I know a potty pause can be frustrating, and you may wonder if there was even any point to practicing EC before this, especially if a potty pause starts to drag on and on. It's really important to stay relaxed and keep in mind that it's normal for children to go through all sorts of challenging phases, not just with elimination but with eating, sleeping, and so on. (Remember, setbacks are normal when conventionally toilet training children, too.) Try to view a potty pause as a positive sign that your child is displaying developmentally appropriate initiative and independence. It also often shows that he has some control over when and where he goes to the bathroom. Later on your child will certainly reach a window of opportunity when all her abilities will be utilized and she desires to use the toilet or potty.

One strategy that worked very well for us whenever we experienced brief potty pauses with our toddlers was to step back almost completely. I would temporarily scale back to offering the potty just once a day at a very reliable time (usually after a nap or before bath), and the rest of the time I would just let things go. Somehow, changing my own mindset and telling myself that it didn't matter was enough to release any tension I might have been feeling over knowing that my child *could* use the potty but had chosen not to. At the same time it gave my child a feeling of control over the situation, and things resolved quickly.

That's what worked for us, but something different may work for your child and your family. I urge you to gather a variety of strategies in your toolbox and go through them all when you come to a rough patch. Almost without fail, parents I've talked to who have gotten through (or never really experienced) potty pauses have put their creative energies to use! They've used strategies such as scaling back, changing locations or potties (for some families, this may mean that the child goes through a phase where he prefers going outdoors or prefers peeing in the bathtub, in a loose diaper, or in a container), or just communicating about wet diapers as often as possible.

Lots of times, especially with a somewhat older toddler who is around, say, sixteen months and up, you can really jump start the process if you stop offering pottytunities and instead trust your child to tell you when he has to go to the bathroom or when he wants to take himself to the bathroom. I've heard of one parent who discovered that all it took for her child to use the toilet again was to let him walk there rather than carry him! Things that seem trivial or simple to us can have tremendous significance in the mind of a child.

Here's another example of how simple changes can make a huge difference and why it's so important to be flexible. My friend Lamelle had put away her Potty Bowls because her daughter, Neshama, hardly seemed to use them now that she was older, preferring her potty instead. Yet suddenly, after a bout of stomach flu when EC went off track, Neshama came upon one of her old Potty Bowls and really took to it. She started preferring the Potty Bowl again and even used it to signal (waving it around in the air). Lamelle figured out that Neshama preferred it for two reasons: using a Potty Bowl allowed her to be snuggled up against her mom (very comforting for a baby just recovering from illness), and she could signal much more dramatically with the Potty Bowl. Had they not stumbled upon the Potty Bowl again, it's quite possible that Neshama would have gone through a prolonged period of misses.

Parents Speak About Toddler Potty Pauses:

Lillian went through a stage at around a year old where she would only use her red Baby Bjorn Little Potty. She also had a stage shortly after this during which she needed all her clothing removed in order to go to the bathroom. We accommodated her seemingly quirky needs even when out and about. I know now that these were both signs of the home stretch to graduation for her at about eighteen months. They were challenging stages, but short-lived, and looking back, these are two very fond and distinct memories that I will always have of her childhood.

—ELIZABETH, MOM OF FIVE, INCLUDING
LILLIAN, 2, AND JACK, 8 MONTHS

Just before Margaret took charge of her toileting, she would refuse to go if I suggested it. Even if she really did have to pee, she wasn't going to the potty if it wasn't her idea! The key then seemed to be for me to just back off and give her the space to take herself to potty. After a week or so of puddles, she was mainly responsible for pee in the potty, and it mostly all went there.

—AMANDA, MOM TO MARGARET, 3

The closest we've been to a potty pause was during the winter, and I attribute it to a difficult adjustment to winter and having to wear pants all the time. Teething causes potty pauses, too. Wally just doesn't signal that reliably at these times. He doesn't resist being taken, but doesn't signal as much, so I use timing.

—SARAH, MOM TO WALLY, 19 MONTHS

After two weeks of EC going really well, my daughter suddenly stopped going for any of my usual and quite varied techniques. I found myself feeling irritated. Why, after proving she could do it, would my daughter stop signaling and stop cooperating? What I realized was that I was not respecting her needs and was wishing to impose my will upon her. I also felt pressure to succeed in this endeavor. Once I came to this insight, I was able to relax, back off, become much more positive, respectful, and communicative, and trust the process. Within a few weeks we were gradually finding ourselves back on track.

—ELLEN, MOM TO CIELO, 6, AND ALEIA, 2

Don't give up. Take a step or two back but don't ditch EC completely. We had potty pauses with both my EC'ed children that started at around nine months and lasted until twelve months. Keep trying the first pee of day, after naps, or even trying different people, places, or receptacles. For instance, my son would only go with daddy for about a month. Also, keep talking about going potty with your child and start working on a sign for potty whenever you take him to the bathroom, he goes, or you have misses. At around twelve months, both of my children learned to make the sign, which made signaling so much easier and helped us out of our potty pause.

—LAURA, MOM TO JEANNINE, 5, BENJAMIN, 3,
AND ROSE, 26 MONTHS

We had a potty pause from about eight months to fourteen months. It ended when Zane became interested in the ASL potty sign and appreciated how fun it was to dump pee out of the potty and so on. Now he signs potty quite frequently, is usually willing to pee in a cup when he is too busy to leave what he is doing (then willingly leaves what he's doing to help carry the pee to the toilet), and tells us consistently when he has to poop (this kind of feels like winning the lottery!).

—KAREN, MOM TO ZANE, 16 MONTHS

We are having a combination of communications and misses. We're having more misses than usual, but Jason is also communicating more readily through sign language, taking off his diaper/training pants/underwear before (or after) going, complaining about being wet, etc. It's an interesting stage.

I find that when I keep track of catches and misses, it's more stressful. I would start to think that I needed to work harder or be more aware. What a headache! Who needs it? Since letting go of my orientation toward results, I've become much more relaxed about practicing EC. The communication I share with Jason has also become more fluid.

—KATHERINE, MOM TO JEFFERSON, 4, AND JASON, 14 MONTHS

We fell out of sync with our daughter for several months from the time she was around twelve to fourteen months. I just cleaned up after her. The hardest part was the poops. She began only pooping while standing up. This lasted a few months. Mostly I left her naked so I could tell when she was starting to poop, and then I'd carry her to the toilet. After a while, things just resolved.

—LISA, MOM TO KAI, 3, AND NOE, 2

If my son has a potty pause, he's almost always dissatisfied with his current situation and is looking for a different potty and/or position. As soon as I provide the experience he's looking for, we get back on track. So I tell people who are going through this to get creative and try something new: Outside? Inside? Toilet insert? Bathtub? Sink? Bowl? Potty? Training pant? Held in position? Clothed, or not? And so forth.

—LAURA, MOM TO JULIAN, 2

At around nine months of age, Jasmine completely rejected the potty. We entered a period of normal diaper use for the next eleven months, but we still felt we had gained a great deal. Following EC had made everything much easier for us in the first nine months. We'd used fewer diapers, and she still maintained her awareness of elimination needs. At twenty months, she suddenly announced that she would not wear diapers anymore. There was no potty training process and she never had an accident.

Overall, EC was a great experience. The savings in time and energy were immense. Even if the only benefit had been avoiding diaper rash (which our first child had), it would have been worth it a million times over to save all the time and stress that went into the trips to the doctor. Similarly, if the only benefit was that Jasmine instantaneously potty trained on her own at one and a half, it would have been worth it because we were finished using diapers at least one year earlier than most children are. We had avoided all the hassles of potty training. But even without those two great bonuses, I still found it saved time and energy to put in the effort up front, practicing EC, rather than after the fact cleaning up dirty diapers and bottoms.

—BRIDGET, MOM TO CARLY, 5, AND JASMINE, 3

Ben goes through phases. Sometimes he likes the potty, sometimes he likes the toilet with a seat, sometimes he likes to be held over the toilet or sink. At times I try all of the above before he goes. And sometimes he's just not in the mood and will not go. Mostly I deal with it by keeping the right attitude. If he goes, great; if he doesn't, he doesn't. I don't look at it as something that I am succeeding or failing at. It's just part of what I do to take care of him, like feeding him and bathing him.

—JULIE, MOM TO BEN, 14 MONTHS

My son's been sick for a couple of weeks, so I try to pee him but not as often as before. He might resist it or arch his back or say no. During the day he's distracted and not feeling well, so we just catch a pee right before he goes to bed.

—HELEN, MOM TO CORWIN, 19 MONTHS

One note: illness might not necessarily throw things off. Parents often wonder how they will EC if their child has a stomach bug, but I've encountered parents whose children actually become fully poop-trained during a bout with mild diarrhea! This happened to us with Benjamin, who caught a stomach flu right after beginning EC. It's almost as if a child becomes hyperaware of the sensation of impending elimination and that this provides a lot of opportunities for "practice." It's so nice for your child not to have all that skin-irritating waste in a diaper!

A FEW STRATEGIES IF YOUR TODDLER EXPERIENCES A POTTY PAUSE

- Change potties or even have your child pee outdoors

- Switch to a toilet insert or potty

- Let your child pick out a new potty

- Change the location of the potty or try a different bathroom if one is available

If your baby is going through a potty pause, taking her to a gathering with other EC'ed babies can help!

- Change your activities while on the potty

- Step back, offer much less, and give your child much more say in initiating pottytunities

- Step up your open-bathroom policy

- Cue your child's dolls or stuffed animals

- Have your child watch an older sibling, friend, or other EC'ed babies use the potty (the latter is particularly effective!)

Parents Share Funny Toddler EC'ing Moments:

Perhaps the most rewarding part of EC'ing a toddler is that it just makes for such amusing moments! It's wonderful to see how delighted they are and to have a window into their world.

> When Wally was eighteen months, we were taking a walk. It was fall. We'd peed outside behind trees and bushes all summer. As we approached a tree, he signed toilet and walked over

expectantly. He peed. Kept walking. Next tree, same thing. Next tree, same thing, except that he was out of pee at this point. Every tree for the whole five blocks and back, he signed potty and marched up like he was going to pee. Apparently, that's just what trees are for!

—SARAH, MOM TO WALLY, 19 MONTHS

We are so open about bodily functions and communicating about elimination that sometimes it makes for funny moments. One time Katie saw a man in a store who had a funny expression on his face, and Katie loudly said, "Man need a potty? Got to poop?" Another time, when I gave a urine sample at the doctor's office, she waited outside with Daddy. The waiting room was packed. I came out, and Katie yelled to me across the room, "Mommy! Wash your hands when you go pee-pee!" Everyone thought it was wildly funny. I assured her I had washed my hands and she told me, "Oh good, Mommy!"

—KELLY, MOM TO KATHLEEN, 2

And, a reminder of why it's good to keep a sense of humor about you . . .

A few weeks ago I heard Isidora and Neve coming out of the bathroom. I'd heard them go in to pee a few minutes earlier and had smiled to myself, thinking how much the kids learn from each other. Now I could hear Isidora saying, "Let's dry our feet off on the carpet." I went to the bathroom. "Why is the floor wet?" "Oh, Neve just made a mistake," Isidora told me, "pouring out the potty." Neve was copying me, trying to pour her pee from the potty to the toilet. Those little toddler arms!

—ANGELA, MOM TO ISIDORA, 3,
AND NEVE, 17 MONTHS

STAYING THE COURSE

Despite the many joys of EC'ing your child, it can sometimes be challenging to stay the course when you run into obstacles along the way. There may be times when it's hard to find the affirmation and encouragement you need to continue this adventurous journey with your little one. There are many parents out there just like you—seek them out! There are so many resources available at your disposal. In the meantime, here are some inspiring thoughts from other parents of EC'ed toddlers:

> I try to approach EC lovingly and with a positive attitude. It's so normal; to us, it's just toilet learning. Just like we teach Willow to use a spoon, to wipe her nose, and to throw a ball, we also teach her about using the potty. And one of the greatest things I've learned is this: anyone can do it and it's adaptable to any lifestyle. You can practice it casually, or you can apply it full-time. EC's not goal-centric, it's more about a learning process. Expect bumps along the road, as with every journey, but don't forget to enjoy the scenery along the way.
>
> —SAM, MOM TO WILLOW, 14 MONTHS

At one point, I was having a hard time, feeling like EC hadn't worked for us, since we missed so many pees. But I was at the park one day with my son and his little friend (who had just started toilet training), and Orlando had to pee, so I took him to the bathroom. After my son peed, I went to offer the little girl the potty and was shocked to find her diaper full of poop, which I hadn't dealt with in a long time. I talked with her about her poop while cleaning her up. At the same time, there was a woman changing her toddler outside the bathroom, continually making sounds of disgust as she held her son's legs up in the air and wiped him.

At that moment, faced with the reality of what it can be like when kids are diapered, I really realized that, while some people think that EC is a lot of work, diapering is not only a lot of work but also means a lot of contact with pee and poop.

—STACY, MOM TO ORLANDO, 30 MONTHS

As parents, we will always have issues and expectations, and EC is good practice for how I want to handle them. For instance, I might think, "I know that he can do this." But in the future, when he is learning to, say, ride a bike, merely telling him, "I know that you can do this" won't be very helpful. I would like to be the kind of parent who helps him overcome any internal blocks or doubts or is simply present to support him as he learns. And I've tried to model that kind of behavior when we have a lot of misses. We did have a potty pause, and he declared he'd rather use a diaper for a while. So we let him use the diaper and continued to offer pottytunities in subtle ways. We also continued, every morning, to offer "underwear or diaper?" without having an expectation of either, like it was a new choice every day and he could decide. For us, that mostly did it. When he went back to underwear, we were back on track.

When we have out-of-sync days, I decide it's because we are not today the persons we were yesterday, and we just need to get back in harmony again as the new and growing people we are now.

—MARIE, MOM TO AIDAN, 29 MONTHS

GRADUATION

What does it mean to have a toilet-trained child? Most conventional definitions include the requirement that a child must be able to complete everything independently, including taking himself to the bathroom and taking off and putting on his own clothes. EC'ers, on the other hand, don't necessarily expect their children to be able to dress themselves or to seat themselves on the toilet to be able to use a toilet, especially for a child who is fully miss-free as a baby or young toddler. If they wait until their children meet that arbitrary requirement, their children might miss out on months or even years exclusively using the toilet for elimination.

In general, an EC "graduate" is a child who is pretty much using the toilet consistently and no longer having misses, or at least not on a regular basis. Parents may still be offering opportunities to the child or accompanying him to the toilet, and in fact, my chats in the bathroom with my sons long provided welcome downtime for us during a hectic day. My friend Laura likens EC graduation with eating; even when a child has completely weaned and is eating solids, he'll still need help cutting up his food. You'll still be monitoring to determine if you should offer him a snack before an outing or to keep his energy up, and so forth. I really like this comparison and find that it helps parents make sense of their continued role in the life of their new EC graduate.

For some EC'ing families, graduation can arrive very quickly. This was the case for our first son. Benjamin went from using diapers full-time to, after a few weeks of intensive diaper-free time and lots of cueing and communicating, being miss-free for good. Others, like my second son, Daniel, arrived at graduation more gradually. While we'd stopped having poop misses during infancy, I'd say that between twelve and seventeen months we had about one to two wet training pants or diapers per day. The last few weeks it was probably a wet diaper every other day or every few days. We arrived at graduation so gradually that I didn't even really notice when it occurred. Neither child experienced regression or any setbacks once they graduated.

There is a range of graduation experiences out there. It's really important, as I state throughout this book, not to be following EC because you want a child who will be potty trained early. While this can definitely happen and is a nice potential side benefit of EC, it is not the point of EC at all and should not be the goal. I would be dismayed if parents who were trying EC felt pressure for their children to graduate by a certain age.

Graduation happens differently for everyone. Some EC'ing families have children who smoothly move into a miss-free lifestyle early in toddlerhood. Others have experiences where the child suddenly becomes miss-free after a long potty pause. Still other families find that their children are not miss-free until about the average age of a conventionally trained child. Chances are that after your child is in underwear or training pants for a while, you will realize that your child is waiting to go to the bathroom or letting you know more often without your needing to offer many pottytunities (unless your child needs a gentle prompt right before going on a long car trip or something like that). No matter what age your child is when he graduates, it's quite likely that you will have been using fewer diapers all along than you would have otherwise, and that your child has been bodily aware for as long as he's been EC'ed—a huge step in becoming toilet-independent.

There are some parents who dislike the very term *graduation* or anything that seems to speak to the expectation that children be toilet trained through this method. They comment that it is often a natural, gradual process with lots of starts and stops and that even having such a concept in mind puts pressure on both parent and child. I understand this feeling. I do find the term handy though because it's good to have a common vocabulary when discussing EC, and it's my hope that once people understand what EC is about, they will realize that it is indeed a gradual process that shouldn't feed any competitive feelings.

Just remember, every child journeys toward toilet independence in his own individual way. As an EC'ing parent, you will be lovingly walking with him and supporting him throughout this process, ready to gently assist him when needed. In a lot of ways, the EC experience mirrors parenthood itself and is really good preparation for so much of what you will encounter later on down the road! EC offers many opportunities for self-reflection and growth. It's like a daily practice in learning how to support your child while also acknowledging, accepting, and celebrating that he is a separate person.

DiaperFreeBaby Cofounder Rachel Milgroom's Thoughts on Graduation

"My experience with EC has been that, like any developmental skill, all children will progress at the rate that's right for them. We started full-time EC at birth with our second son, and he was about two and a half years old when he could reliably go through the day without any wet underwear. He was a full three years old before we could dependably leave the house without a "just in case" change of clothes.

A child learning to manage his or her own elimination needs is engaging in a process like any other learning they do. The more present we parents are with our children, the more rewarding it is for both parents and children. Through my experience of having a child who was dependably dry on the later end of the EC spectrum, I found that I had to move away from the culturally ingrained "first is better" competitive mentality. By accepting my son's schedule, I experienced a profound mental and emotional transition that allowed me to let go of pressured expectations of myself and my children. And my son did get to a place where he was dependably dry, on a timetable that suited his needs."

Parents Speak about the Road to Graduation:

Among families who EC, the goal is *not* potty training. Rather, it's to learn and respond to your child's signals (using the diaper as a backup and the potty as the primary place to eliminate). Ever so gradually, your child takes over responsibility for the task. It's very relaxed, pressure-free, and such an everyday occurence that you never really go through "potty training" as you usually think of it in this society. It's strikingly similar to the transition from breastfeeding exclusively to introducing solid foods to gradually being able to eat "independently."

—MEGAN, MOM TO NOEMI, 30 MONTHS

When our son was almost two years old, he had been poop trained for a year and we'd had no misses. Pees were a different story. He always told us right as or after he went, but we were missing as many as we were catching. I was starting to feel anxious; after all, we had been doing this for a long time and I think I had unconsciously expected him to be "done" by two years of age. I could feel this tension creeping into our relationship and he even stopped telling us about his pees. I was feeling even more frustrated because it felt like he was backsliding! Whenever I catch myself having these thoughts about my child in regard to anything—peeing, talking, climbing, whatever—it is a very clear sign to me to let go. So that is what I did. I stopped asking him if he had to go, stopped checking his pants for pee, and stopped offering the potty.

Within a month he was telling us about his pees again, and shortly after that he told us about them beforehand, reliably. At two years and one month, he graduated.

—STACY, MOM TO ORLANDO, 30 MONTHS

When Samuel was about eighteen months, he was on the verge of graduating. He had about three weeks with no misses, then a little period of backsliding and misses. At around twenty-one months he "graduated"—I didn't have to think about his elimination very much, and he could take himself to the bathroom by himself, minus some clothing help or help getting on the toilet if it was high.

—MELINDA, MOM TO SAMUEL, 3,
AND HANNAH, 10 MONTHS

Margaret graduated so gradually that it was pretty unnoticed. We had a potty in the main room and dressed Margaret in elastic-waist pants that she could maneuver. At around sixteen to seventeen months, she would refuse to pee if I suggested it, even if she really had to go and had a miss a few minutes later. I think she wanted me to back off, so that she could be the one to decide when she needed to pee. Once I backed off and stopped asking, we had puddles for a few days or weeks and then she was consistently taking herself to the potty without even consulting me or asking my help.

—AMANDA, MOM TO MARGARET, 3

With my daughter, EC was such a non-issue. There was no pressure for her and she just "graduated" in her own time, at around twenty-four to twenty-five months. I still help her in the bathroom at times, but she tells me when she wants to go and I don't even think about it anymore. Most kids her age are still wearing diapers. I'm so happy we followed EC and gave our kids this freedom and dignity.

—LISA, MOM TO KAI, 3, AND NOE, 2

THE END OF ONE JOURNEY IS ONLY THE BEGINNING OF ANOTHER

Eventually, your baby will be completely toilet-independent and your EC'ing days will be behind you. You'll put your potties, training pants, and fleece pads away, perhaps with a bit of nostalgia. It doesn't matter what age your baby is when she is fully out of diapers; the journey to this place in your child's life will have been an amazing one when you look back at it. You made the decision to be responsive, to be present, and to be open-minded and receptive to all that your child was communicating. There is no doubt in my mind that you and your child will continue to benefit from the foundation of trust and communication that you've built together and the lessons you've learned through EC. Congratulations!

9.

If Your Situation Is a Little Different

If you're reading this chapter, you may feel that your situation isn't as straightforward as those of the other families described in this book. Perhaps you have a premature baby, a child with special needs, or an older child whom you want to toilet train using EC principles. You may be working while your child is in day care, or you may have multiples, or you may be toilet training an older child conventionally while also desiring to practice EC with your younger baby. Read on for more information about special situations such as yours.

EC AND WORKING PARENTS

One of the most important messages about EC that I tell parents is that EC to any degree is still EC. That's why I placed such emphasis on the part-time and occasional EC categories in previous chapters. Applying EC part-time, especially when you're just starting out, takes pressure off parents and helps them realize that EC is truly achievable. Needless to say, part-time EC can be especially appropriate for working parents.

Many working parents love the way that EC fosters another

connection between them and their child during the time they have together. If their child is with an open-minded caregiver, they may encourage the caregiver to form his or her own EC relationship with the child. Other parents may choose that their children be conventionally diapered during the week and EC'ed only during evenings or weekends.

Some working parents prioritize full-time EC during the time they have together with their child because they feel it's even more crucial to provide a consistent environment when their time at home is limited. Parents who work may also make other adjustments if they can—similar to what they might do when establishing a healthy nursing relationship with a newborn baby—such as stretching out parental leave as long as possible so that the family can get off to a good EC'ing start, juggling schedules so that the baby is with one parent as much as possible during the first few months of life, and arranging to be with the baby during lunch breaks.

By the way, a large percentage of the parents I've quoted throughout this book are working parents, so be sure to reread anecdotes from previous chapters as well.

Parents Speak About Working and EC:

Zane changes a lot during the week, and I'm not always aware of those changes. For a long time I thought he still occasionally peed at twenty-minute intervals, until one weekend I just observed him without worrying about catching pees. Lo and behold, it turned out he could hold it much longer than that!

—KAREN, MOM TO ZANE, 19 MONTHS

Once Betsy was sixteen months, she would walk toward the potty and lift up her shirt when she had to go—a very clear signal. When her day-care providers saw that she was using the potty, we started sending her there in underwear. They were also willing to let us bring in a potty for her.

—EMILY, MOM TO BETSY, 2

We each toilet the baby equally, and I think that is the secret to success with dual working parents. Both parents must see the value of it and contribute to the effort because both parents are probably equally spent when they get home from work. Success also comes from being consistent—for us that meant all time away from day care was diaper-free/EC time. The more we did it, the more we realized how convenient EC was compared to diaper wearing.

When Felix was seven to twelve months old and in institutional day-care, our routine was the same every day. My husband would offer him the toilet at home, then drive to the day care, take Felix to the toilet there, diaper him, and leave. I'd arrive at lunch, check him and change him immediately, nurse, take him to the toilet, and go back to work. After work I would go to the day care, take the diaper off immediately, clean him up, nurse him, and again offer the toilet. Even if he didn't go, I wanted him to know that he would always have the opportunity. I used my wrap to tie him on my back while heading home on the subway. As soon as I got home, I'd take him off my back and potty him. In five months of doing this, he never once wet or soiled my back but would immediately go as soon as I put him on the toilet at home. I had no doubt that he knew exactly what was going on and was holding it until we got home.

When Felix was older and I realized his current (institutional) day care was not working for him, I began to seriously research home day-cares as an alternative. I wanted to find someone who would EC with him because I wanted him to feel that his caregiver was attentive and responsive to his communication. I phone screened about fifteen different providers and found one who seemed genuinely interested and supportive. At thirteen months, I switched him to this new provider, who has cared for him ever since. She very quickly got the hang of EC'ing him, which I think earned his trust and helped him to adjust.

—KAREN, MOM TO FELIX, 17 MONTHS

One Working Mom's EC Tips

Laura Hamilton, mother of Julian, twenty-two months, has written a primer on combining work and EC. Here are a few of her tips and strategies:

- I pottied my baby upon first waking in the morning, and thereafter as frequently as I thought he might have to go until I had to leave for work. (Use diaper-free time on weekends to get a good estimate of how often your baby usually has to eliminate.)

- When we arrived at the day care, I took my son to the toilet one last time before leaving. I would also potty him very first thing at the day care upon arriving to pick him up (this can save you a wet diaper on the way home!). My son never got confused by this. He seemed to accept and understand that Mama would take him potty, but the caregivers at day care would not.

- Apart from wake-up pees, I would offer "pottytunities" at every diaper change when my baby was already diaper-free. This is a great habit to get into for part-timers using diaper backup. It helps you avoid the common problems of being peed or pooped on at the changing table or having your baby immediately go to the bathroom in a fresh diaper.

- It's also a good idea to have baby in a cloth diaper without a cover (or training pants or underwear) at home. That way you can tell very quickly when your baby has peed. The baby will also get physical feedback from a pee. I used disposables as a backup, but I stopped at around one year old. I realized that I tended to ignore my son's potty signals when he was diapered in a disposable. However, do whatever makes you most comfortable and relaxed in the process! Feel free to use a diaper backup. Just keep taking the diaper off to offer the potty on a regular basis.

- Dress your baby in loose sweatpants or something easy to take off for ease of pottying—no one-piece outfits with snaps. They make it such a pain to get the clothes off that you tend to just leave your baby in the diaper until it's full.

That's it! EC is easy and anyone can do it. It's not an all-or-nothing practice. Why not give pottying a try tomorrow morning at diaper change time and see what happens?

EC AND THE PREMATURE BABY

DiaperFreeBaby Mentors often get requests from parents of premature infants who are wondering if EC is feasible for them. It certainly is; the most common rule of thumb is not to begin until the baby comes home from the hospital or is at or past her adjusted due date. Because preterm babies often spend the first period of their lives in an NICU, it's difficult and unnecessary for parents to spend time trying to keep their infants diaper-free before they come home. When ready, proceed according to the other sections of the book, depending on when you decide to begin.

One Indian friend told me that many Indians start EC as soon as a baby can hold her head up on her own, so that is what we did with our premature baby (born at twenty-six weeks). She was developmentally about two months when we started EC. In other words, she was two months, adjusted (two months past the date she was supposed to have been due).

—ASMIRA, MOM TO VEDA, 16 MONTHS

EC AND MULTIPLES

We often get requests from parents of multiples who are hoping to keep the channels of communication open between themselves and their babies in hopes of avoiding the task of conventionally toilet training two or three children all at once. They may also be motivated to save money by using fewer diapers.

Naturally, parents of multiples often feel daunted by EC. But I do know families who have incorporated it into their lives with success. In fact, the first time I ever saw EC practiced was when I was living with a host family in Japan. My host mother had twin baby granddaughters, and one day I saw her take the babies, one at a time, and cue them while holding them over a bowl! It was astonishing to me. Clearly, she didn't feel that it was impossible to EC twins.

Remember that the situation varies from family to family. It's not terribly different to EC multiples part-time than it is to change several diapers on two or more babies a day. It's important to be aware of what you can handle whether you are EC'ing a singleton or multiples. That's why I emphasize EC to any degree—the degree that's right for you—throughout this book.

One of my close friends, Emily, is EC'ing twins. When they were first born, I told her that she did not need to feel pressure; there was plenty of time in the future to devote to EC. Plenty of windows of opportunity would certainly occur. But by following EC casually (by, for instance, cueing them while they pooped in a diaper, or simply by staying aware of their patterns), she was ensuring that she'd be open to those windows of opportunity when they came again.

When EC'ing multiples, it's important to remember that your children are separate people, and that their development is most likely going to be different in every way. They are going to pass through all the stages of EC, and graduate, at their own individual pace. Be extra careful to be matter-of-fact about EC'ing so that the children don't feel compared. Remember to have one potty for each child, and consider pottying them one at a time or pottying them separately so that they do not become confused if you are cueing one and not the other. (As they get older, this sort of confusion will be less of an issue.)

A Parent Speaks About EC'ing Twins:

> I have practiced EC with my girls since birth. At first I wasn't really sure it would work. My girls are very different in temperament and body type. Tsameret will cry out sharply when something bothers her. Moriah is more of an observer, but physically precocious. She is apt to pee while standing and will come to me with her pants already wet, while Tsameret is more likely to cry before she feels the urge to eliminate and come to me to catch her pees. Thus, EC'ing goes differently for each of them. But both girls are pretty much in sync when it comes to eating and sleeping, and so it goes for elimination as well. Often one will pee and the other will pee a split second later. I've learned, instead of cleaning after one pee right away, to look for the other girl and try to catch hers.
>
> EC'ing with twins has not been an easy or smooth process because there is always the problem of not being able to tend to one while occupied with the other, especially in the early months. However, the advantage is that as they get older, they learn from each other!

After six months, they stopped signaling for a time. Eventually, we pretty much went diaperless because of diaper rash and other issues. Now they wear cotton or wool pants, and their signals have become much clearer!

As imperfect as our system is, it does seem as if we're communicating and getting through to each other, and that is tremendously rewarding.

—LUCIA, MOM TO MORIAH AND
TSAMERET, 9 MONTHS

Although EC'ing twins can be challenging, the advantage is that babies learn from each other as they grow.

EC'ING A CHILD WITH DISABILITIES

EC is helpful for children with disabilities, and I've spoken to several parents who are grateful to have practiced EC with their children because it helped them retain bodily awareness and provided a valuable means of communication between parent and child. Dr. Emily Davidson, an EC'ing mom and a pediatric instructor at Harvard Medical School who cares for children with complex medical problems and developmental disabilities, remarks, "If you have a child who has some developmental disability, milestones may not appear in the same order and your child may not hit the same milestones as typically developing children—so this is a barrier to using conventional toilet training methods. A child who might never walk or talk won't use the same signals, so you have to use a different approach anyway. One of the things that many parents of kids with disabilities find is that they spend a lot of time observing their children and become very attuned to their children's needs in general. I think the benefit of EC is that you could potentially introduce toileting at a much younger age than you would if you were waiting. You're helping them to learn about their bodies and the parts of their bodies they can control." Davidson also points out, "Some of the things that are true of EC in general are extra true when EC'ing a child with disabilities. Don't set yourself a time frame and don't get overly caught up in success. Rather, focus more on the process of teaching your child to identify his need to use the toilet."

Parents Speak About EC'ing a Child with Special Needs:

A lot of people with disabilities who are in wheelchairs and who are not verbal may be in diapers forever. Aidan, who has cerebral palsy, may not become toilet-independent till he's older, but I'm really glad that we've maintained his connection to his bodily awareness. EC also provides him with another opportunity to communicate with us. He uses body language and signals; I can tell when he needs to go.

—PAMELA, MOM TO AIDAN, 2

Jonathan, our third child, was born with Down syndrome. We were living in China at the time. We observed what other parents in China were doing and decided to follow our own modified plan of what they did. Since we both work full-time, we hired a Chinese nanny to help take care of the baby. Within a few weeks, he would pee when he heard a *"shhhing"* sound. Because he has gross motor delays, he can't walk by himself or get onto a toilet seat by himself, so we take him regularly. Going to the bathroom is a fun time for him. Jonathan learned to regularly use the toilet for urinating and defecating by the time he was one year old. His older brother and sister didn't learn to do this until they were three and two years old. So even though Jonathan is delayed in so many other areas, this is something he is advanced in and can feel good about when he is older.

—RANDY AND KAREN, PARENTS TO JONATHAN, 2

EC'ING THE OLDER CHILD

In general, EC is best practiced with babies and young infants. Inevitably, however, many parents come to DiaperFreeBaby looking for information about introducing the toilet to their older, often resistant, children in as loving, respectful, and empathetic a manner as possible. While most of the principles of EC are indeed geared toward younger children, they can be adapted to the older child as well.

Reread chapters 6 and 7 on EC'ing an older baby or toddler. The significant, additional step for both those stages is to let your baby experience wetness or elimination by giving her diaper-free time (or time in a cloth diaper or training pant). This is an important first step with your older toddler. Make sure that she has the opportunity to feel what it is like to actually pee. After two to three years of peeing in a diaper, it's more than likely that she is no longer conscious of the sensation of peeing, or that she's tuned it out. Reawaken this feeling in her for a few days, perhaps restricting diaperless time to outdoors or to certain periods of the day and certain locations in the house if that would work better for you.

The cornerstone of EC is, of course, communication, and this is just as important with an older child. Use communication to help your child make associations between certain cues or words and going to the bathroom.

Understand that your child is attempting to switch gears after years of developing a reliance on her diaper and that this can be distressing or difficult. (It may not be, but parents of older children are usually drawn to EC because conventional toilet training techniques have failed.) Put yourself in her place and understand that it takes some time to figure out which muscles to use to release in a certain position.

With an older child, learning to poop in the toilet rather than in the diaper he's been accustomed to can sometimes be a difficult experience. If he is actually withholding stool in order to put off pooping in the potty or toilet, this can lead to a painful cycle of constipation, pain, more withholding, and a negative association with the toilet. Address the constipation first by making appropriate changes to his diet. Be very understanding of his reluctance to change the pattern he is used to, and respect his pace so that he can remain comfortable. It can be helpful at first to encourage him to poop in the bathroom—near the potty or toilet—even if he is actually pooping in his diaper, or to let him poop on the toilet while wearing a diaper. Keep talking to him about elimination and invite him to give the potty a try when he feels ready.

Make bathroom time fun, and let your child enjoy the bonding experience of spending time with you as she experiments with the toilet. Let her know you are on her side. Above all, stay relaxed.

An older child will often enjoy picking out her own potties, picking out her own underwear, and so forth, so be sure to involve her in the process.

We actually tried EC when our son Charlie was about nine months old, but never stuck with it long enough for him to regain any bodily awareness. He'd sit on the potty but not go, so we stopped. When he was three, and starting to want to use the potty himself, he'd sit on one but again, no awareness, so no results. So we started trying to dress him in cotton briefs every morning after breakfast. Each day when he'd wet himself, we'd try to acknowledge it *as* he was peeing. Once he made the connection with the feeling of releasing pee with peeing, he was quickly able to gain body control and began using the potty regularly for pees.

—LARRY, DAD TO CHARLIE, 3

We sometimes hear from people with older children who want to attend a DiaperFreeBaby meeting. I make sure the parent understands that in general, EC begins with a much younger baby, and the focus of the group and experience of most members will reflect that, but I then point out that a lot of the general suggestions can be applied at older ages as well, such as those involving communication, give and take, and creativity. Then I let the parent decide. I think we find that a lot of parents gain insight for their situations from the group no matter how old their children are.

—AMANDA, MOM TO MARGARET, 3

EC'ING TWO AT ONCE

It's not at all uncommon for us to meet families who are practicing EC with a younger baby while simultaneously trying to train an older sibling. There are also many cases of families who are finishing up EC with a toddler in addition to caring for a newborn EC'ed baby. If this is your situation, know that you're in good company. It may initially seem as if it would be totally overwhelming to do this, many families actually find that working with the two children at the same time has benefits for both children. The older siblings often get a jump start when they realize their baby brother or sister is also using a potty, and they can be very involved in helping out with EC tasks—bringing a potty, cueing, etc. This also gives you an opportunity to talk about pottying, and the more you talk about pottying and elimination, the better. Finally, your younger baby, as he grows, will increasingly enjoy the chance to sit on the potty alongside his older sibling.

Parents Speak About Strategies When Two Children Are Toilet Learning:

I learned to offer the potty to the toddler before my newborn or else my toddler would pee while waiting for the baby to potty. I even started carrying both a little potty and a potty bowl when out for long periods of time so the children could potty at the same time. It wasn't overwhelming. I loved that almost all poops were in a potty, not a diaper.

—KEILA, MOM TO JANE, 27 MONTHS,
AND HELEN, 8 MONTHS

My first son was potty trained conventionally. I started at twenty-seven months and it took a good three months before he was reliably clean and dry. I did think how strange it was that I'd conditioned him into using diapers, then switched to a potty. During this time I discovered EC. I had been putting four-month-old baby Oliver on the potty to encourage Jonathan to use it, and to my surprise he'd often pee when I did this. From then on I was hooked and convinced that EC was a far more appropriate and gentle method for toilet learning. Now Jonathan enjoys signing "potty" to Oliver and loves to help out whenever he can!

—KEZ, MOM TO JONATHAN, 3,
AND OLIVER, 8 MONTHS

Even before learning about EC, I instinctively put my son on the potty to poop when he was seven months old, but only for a few weeks because I was intimidated when someone told me that children really aren't ready until they are at least eighteen months old. I stopped because I was worried I'd done something wrong. However, I think the experience stayed with him because when we did start potty training, he seemed to remember, although there were some power struggles about it. Ironically, he eventually trained just after his second birthday, after he saw his baby sister peeing on the potty and recognized all the positive reinforcement associated with it. She's been EC'ed since three months.

—CARRIE, MOM TO CONNOR, 3,
AND RILEY, 17 MONTHS

Bekah was twenty-six months old and conventionally diapered when Lillian was born. Lillian was EC'ed full-time from birth, so it was fascinating to watch them learn and grow together. Sometimes their toilet learning was remarkably similar at certain stages, though they were more than two years apart.

—ELIZABETH, MOM TO FIVE, INCLUDING
BEKAH, 5, LILLIAN, 2, AND JACK, 8 MONTHS

These are just a few of the many special situations you may encounter. Each family and child is unique. Many more tips on specific situations can be found if you join online or real-life support groups (see the resources at the end of the book).

FINAL WORDS

Congratulations for embarking on your EC journey! No matter how far you've come or how you've decided to integrate EC into your life, I applaud you all. Like so much else in parenting, the art of EC involves balance. Each moment of each day, you are balancing the needs of your child, your family, and yourself. You have recognized that practicing EC offers a unique opportunity to nurture your child's well-being and happiness, starting in babyhood—a brief period of time that is as infinitely precious as it is heartbreakingly fleeting.

Every child and every family is different. The range of experiences among EC'ing families reflects this diversity. Remember that staying relaxed, gathering support and nurturing yourself, and listening to your baby will put you on a sure path toward parenting with joy and happiness. It's my hope that your willingness to listen and respond to your young child by practicing EC will provide a solid foundation for the many parenting adventures that await you and your family in the future.

RESOURCES

For the most updated information on EC and other responsive parenting practices, see the author's website at www.thediaperfree baby.com

GEAR

Diapers, underwear, and EC clothing

www.theECstore.com (a wide selection of EC gear—diapers, training pants, underwear, EC clothing—including split-crotch pants and BabyLegs—PULpads, Baby Bjorn potties and toilet reducers, Babywunder Deluxe Clear Potties, Potty Bowls, potty warmers, and other items)

www.wonderbabydesigns.com (Poquito Pants™ baby underwear)

www.babyworks.com (cloth diapers and training pants, wool puddle pads)

www.diaperware.com (large selection of cloth diapers and accessories)

www.underthenile.com (organic cotton diapers and training pants)

www.hannaandersson.com (xs boys and girls underwear and training pants)

www.fuzzibunz.com—Fuzzi Bunz pocket diapers

www.kissaluvs.com—fitted, snap cotton diapers

www.bumkins.com—all-in-one (AIO) cloth diapers
www.gap.com (xxs cotton underwear)
www.babylegs.net (website of the creator of BabyLegs—leggings
    for the EC'ed baby)
www.diaperfreebaby.org/shop (EC items available from
    DiaperFreeBaby)

Babywearing

www.kangarookorner.com (slings and baby carriers)
www.peppermint.com (slings and baby carriers)
www.thebabywearer.com (online baby-wearing resource center)
www.nineinnineout.org (NINO) (baby-wearing advocacy site)
www.mamatoto.org (baby-wearing advocacy site with
    comprehensive list of baby-wearing support groups
    and classes)

WEBSITES ABOUT ELIMINATION COMMUNICATION

www.DiaperFreeBaby.org
www.timl.com/ipt/
www.natural-wisdom.com
www.PottyWhisperer.com
www.commtechlab.msu.edu/sites/aslweb/browser.htm (a site that
    demonstrates American Sign Language signs, including the
    "toilet sign" [under *T*])

ONLINE SUPPORT GROUPS

http://groups.yahoo.com/group/eliminationcommunication/
    (elimination communication discussion group)
http://groups.yahoo.com/group/NaturalInfantHygiene/ (natural
    infant hygiene discussion group)
http://groups.yahoo.com/group/IPTLateStarters/ (infant potty

training for "late-starters"—babies over six months of age when starting EC)

www.mothering.com/discussions/([Mothering Dot Commune EC bulletin board] Visit the elimination communication forum under *Diapering*)

PUBLICATIONS ABOUT EC

Bauer, Ingrid. *Diaper Free! The Gentle Wisdom of Natural Infant Hygiene.* NY: *Plume (Penguin), 2006.*

Boucke, Laurie. *Infant Potty Basics: With or Without Diapers . . . The Natural Way.* Lafayette, CO: White-Boucke Publishing, 2003.

———. *Infant Potty Training: A Gentle and Primeval Method Adapted to Modern Living.* Lafayette, CO: White-Boucke Publishing, 2002.

Natec, *Elimination Timing: The Solution to the Dirty Diapers War.* Kea'au, Hawaii, 1994.

PARENTING SUPPORT

www.attachmentparenting.org (website of Attachment Parenting International, a nonprofit clearinghouse that provides support groups and resources to promote Attachment Parenting)

www.lalecheleague.org (website of La Leche League International, an organization that provides mother-to-mother support, education, and information about breastfeeding)

www.askdrsears.com (general advice on parenting and health care by Dr. William Sears, M.D., author and pediatrician)

www.findothermoms.com (finds moms near you who share similar interests and parenting philosophies)

ACKNOWLEDGMENTS

This book would never have existed without the unwavering support of two amazing women and mothers: Melinda Rothstein and Rachel Milgroom, cofounders of DiaperFreeBaby. Our meetings and discussions have taught me so much about motherhood and being in tune with my babies. Melinda and Rachel's dream of helping to influence how we parent our babies by raising awareness of EC has come true, and I'm honored to be part of their endeavors.

I'm truly grateful to Talia Cohen, my agent, who had faith in this project—and my writing—from the very start. Without her constant encouragement and straight thinking, this book would never have come to fruition.

Judith Regan, my editor Maureen O'Neal, and Jenny Brown, all of Regan, were a pleasure to work with and invaluable for guiding this book through to the end.

Laurie Boucke has been an inspiration and a supportive friend. She answered one of my questions on an online bulletin board when my first son went through a brief "potty pause." Her sensible advice helped us to stay the course when I had no one else to ask. Ingrid Bauer, another EC author, was a gracious presence in my life. Laurie's and Ingrid's work in helping to raise awareness of diaper-free babies helped a book like mine to become a reality, and I am grateful to them.

I thank my parents Charles and Hwasun Loh, for always believing in me and encouraging me no matter what I pursued. They quietly and unfailingly support my parenting, which is the best gift any daughter could have, and they are such loving grandparents. If my mother, unfettered by cultural norms, had not gently persisted in giving me a potty when my son was a baby, we never even would have begun this journey. That they were unsurprised (but delighted nonetheless) by the idea of diaper-free babies led us to where we are now.

I'm grateful to my brother Lawrence Loh for bringing laughter and music to all our lives. His lovely wife, Jennifer, and children, Charlie and Hilary, are precious members of our family. As this book went to press we were excited to see that baby Hilary was happily using the potty. This is the greatest testament to their belief in this project.

I heartily thank my brother Dan Loh, both for initially nudging me to write this book and for being such an integral part of this project by using his prodigious photographic talents toward a new end: capturing diaper-free babies on film—not an easy task! His patience and his willingness to lead multiple shoots and dedicate hours to photo editing directly resulted in fabulous images for this book and my website.

Thanks to Amy Miller, as well, for assisting Dan so ably in his work and for helping me out with just about everything when I was scrambling around writing this book. Her gentle, helpful presence smoothed the path so I could concentrate on what I needed to do.

Much thanks to my in-laws, Phil, Laurie, Amy, and Julie Gross, and Leslie and Kenny Klaff, and my adorable nieces and nephews Jacob, Emma, Brandon, and Zoe. They have provided constant support and love throughout the years, and our boys are blessed to have them in their lives. No daughter- or sister-in-law could be luckier than to have such a loving, open-minded extended family. I thank Grandma Ida, too, for being my special cheerleader—her love means a lot to me.

And much, much loving thanks to my husband, David Gross-

Loh, for being a wonderful husband and father. I'm blessed to be sharing the parenting journey with him. Seeing what a naturally intuitive and empathetic parent he is strengthens the love we have for our sons and each other.

I'm fortunate to have friends like Lamelle Ryman and Laura Simeon, and thank them for their insightful edits and close readings of the manuscript in its initial stages. I have the greatest respect both for their amazing editorial skills and for the loving parents they are. Watching Laura parent her daughter well before my children were born planted a seed and showed me what kind of mother I would want to become someday. Watching Lamelle experience new motherhood after my children were past babyhood reminded me of where my children and I have come from and how important it is to always honor the precious foundations set during infancy.

I thank my dear friend Yun Wolfe, whose insights always anticipate where I'm heading next. Her common sense advice to follow Benjamin's lead on the toilet, rather than wait until he was older, provided me with yet more support for an unorthodox path.

Thanks to Ashisha, of *Mothering* magazine, for giving me my first writing break and the opportunity to write on meaningful topics close to my heart.

To the women of my August 2000 Babies online support group—our constant conversations over the years have deepened and refined my views on parenting and life. Without the privilege of knowing so many women of different backgrounds and outlooks, my views would not have matured in the way that they have.

I'm truly grateful to Kanako Hirano for having been such a loving part of our family for important years of my children's early lives. Without her help and the love she provides our boys, my career would never have gotten off the ground.

I appreciate Lara Goodman, Kate Twelker, Erin Miner, Dara Freed, Haya Brandt, Vanessa Rudin, and all the other members of our NYC DiaperFreeBaby group. I thank them for their faithful attendance at our meetings and the way they've helped spread the word about EC.

Through reading manuscript drafts, tossing ideas around, and online brainstorming late into the night, Marie Pechet, Elizabeth Parise, Amanda Alvine, and Katherine Abbey provided me with a constant stream of encouragement when I was putting this book together, and they helped give me confidence that my message was on target. Their generous work for DiaperFreeBaby and their support for my book is much appreciated.

To all my photo models: wonderful moms and dads . . . and babies adorable beyond words. My greatest thanks to them for being so willing to help spread the word by trekking out to my place for multiple photo shoots and letting us capture their beautiful babies on film.

And finally, I am appreciative of the many moms and dads who contributed so much to this book by providing wonderfully detailed testimonials of their EC'ing experience. I was fortunate to have so many enthusiastic and articulate parents to talk to, and I was impressed by the depth of their insights into EC, parenting, and all else. This book has grown out of all the things they've taught me—I thank them for giving me such an intimate glimpse into their lives and thoughts. Ultimately, I have only been a conduit for the wisdom they generously and eagerly opted to share. This book, filled with their voices and shaped by their experiences, really belongs to them.

INDEX

NOTES

NOTES

NOTES

NOTES

NOTES

NOTES

NOTES

NOTES